ANIMAL AMAZING

BOOKS by JUDITH HERBST

Sky Above and Worlds Beyond
Bio Amazing
Animal Amazing

ANIMAL AMAZING
JUDITH HERBST

ATHENEUM   1991   NEW YORK

COLLIER MACMILLAN CANADA
Toronto
MAXWELL MACMILLAN INTERNATIONAL PUBLISHING GROUP
New York • Oxford • Singapore • Sydney

The author wishes to thank William R. Corliss
for his perceptive reading of the manuscript
and his useful suggestions.

Atheneum
Macmillan Publishing Company
866 Third Avenue, New York, NY 10022

Collier Macmillan Canada, Inc.
1200 Eglinton Avenue East
Suite 200
Don Mills, Ontario M3C 3N1

First Edition
Printed in the United States of America
10 9 8 7 6 5 4 3 2 1

Library of Congress Cataloging-in-Publication Data
Herbst, Judith.
  Animal amazing / by Judith Herbst.
     p.   cm.
  Summary: Examines the amazing world of animals, from the feats of
ordinary dogs to unproved monsters in the wild.
  ISBN 0-689-31556-2
1. Animals—Miscellanea—Juvenile literature. [1. Animals.]
I. Title.
QL49.H53   1991   591—dc20
90–62 CIP   AC

FOR
JONATHAN GREENFIELD, D.V.M, MASTER SURGEON,
NURSE FRAN AND MARIBETH,
AND BRIDGET M. BROOKE, V.M.D,
THE REAL DR. DOOLITTLE

I never saw a purple cow,
I never hope to see one;
But I can tell you anyhow,
I'd rather see than be one.

     Gelett Burgess

Contents

CHAPTER 1

My Dog, the Fortune-Teller

Before there were scientists, before there were humans even, there were the animals. They evolved from single cells when all life on Earth looked pretty much the same. Through trial and error, the animals adapted, and as the millennia passed, they developed a core of responses to the earth that would ensure their survival. Many birds and others sensitive to the deep cold made it through the winter by migrating on a yearly basis to warmer climates. Others hibernated. Furbearers grew thicker, more protective coats. As the earth shifted, so did the animals.

If all this does not make animals considerably smarter than us, it does give them more experience. For instance, when sparrows start urgently chirping and spiraling upward, you might want to consider taking along your umbrella. No, the sparrows don't know anything about low pressure systems and advancing fronts. They can't tell the difference between an isobar and a candy bar, but they are able to sense subtle changes in the atmosphere, changes that herald rain, snow, and even approaching fog.

Indeed, anecdotes abound about how animals seem to have predicted storms and hurricanes. Fisherman William Montgomery tells a rather impressive dog tale about his setter, Redsy, who absolutely refused one day to board Montgomery's flounder boat. Since puppyhood, Redsy had been an avid fisher-dog, always gleeful at the prospect of a day on the water. But despite the promise of a spectacular sunrise and the scores of fishing boats already chugging away from the harbor, Redsy resisted all of Montgomery's efforts to get him on the boat. Barking furiously and crouching at the far end of the pier, Redsy made his feelings quite obvious: No fishing!

Montgomery admitted later that Redsy's strange behavior had made him feel a little uneasy, so he decided to skip fishing that day. There was certainly no other reason to stay ashore; the sky was deep blue and cloudless, with scarcely a breeze. But Redsy had been so insistent. . . .

It was early afternoon when the wind rose. It came up suddenly and with a vengeance, tearing at the trees and churning the glass-calm waters. Storm waves forty feet high ripped out of the sea and rolled inexorably toward shore. And then came the rains, driving and slashing and heralding the arrival of the great hurricane of 1938. When it was over, many fishing boats had been claimed by the waves, and six hundred people had lost their lives.

Montgomery never doubted for a minute that Redsy's "radar" about the impending storm had saved both their lives. He called it Redsy's "subtle canine senses," and indeed, that's exactly what it may have been. As the data pour in from eyewitnesses, more and more animals reveal their remarkable clairvoyant abilities. No, they cannot predict what the stock market will do or whether you will marry someone rich, but if you live in earthquake country, the family dog may just be able to tell your fortune.

The story of the animals and the earthquakes begins deep inside the earth where the temperatures are high enough to keep the rock flowing like hot tar. Earth's land masses are constantly in motion. They sit on plates, which are like ferryboats, riding over the earth's surface, moving only inches each year. But the plates have very little room to maneuver. As a matter of fact, they are jammed together so tightly, it is a wonder they can move at all. But move they do, slip-sliding past each other like subway commuters during rush hour.

There are times, however, when two plates become so tightly wedged together that they barely can budge. Months pass. Then years. Then decades. But the plates remain stuck, and all the while, the stresses are building. And then one day the earth snaps, and the plates pull away with a mighty grunch! The land high above cracks like a saltine, and the planet suffers what is aptly called an earthquake.

In the part of the earth that is California, an enormous crack opens in the seafloor like some prehistoric monster. The crack hugs the shoreline as it travels downward to the San Francisco peninsula. It then veers east toward Los Angeles, a highly populated city that has the extreme misfortune to be sitting upon a vast network of cracks, all courtesy of the main break. The total distance traveled by California's great crack is some 650 miles, an accomplishment that should have earned it the name El Longo, but it is called instead the San Andrea Fault. You may have heard of it.

People blame the San Andreas Fault for every tremor in the state, and some even have tried to pin Alaskan and Mexican quakes on it. But while the San Andreas is the best-known fault, it is hardly the only one in the area. The entire western coast of the United States is loaded with faults (geologic ones, that is), and they are all part of what scientists have identified as the "ring of fire."

If you plot the areas on the earth that are prone to major earthquakes, you will get something roughly resembling a great circle extending from the Pacific coast of South America, up through Mexico, the western coast of the United States, Canada, and Alaska, across the Bering Sea, down into Japan, the Philippines, New Guinea, and the islands of the South Pacific, and around into New Zealand. Since most of these areas are also associated with volcanoes, the term "ring of fire" becomes very appropriate.

Despite the enormous area covered by the ring of fire, most of earth's billions have no firsthand experience with earthquakes. They know them only as a series of pictures on a TV screen, and even then, it is long after the fact, when searchers are already digging through the rubble for bodies, or bulldozers are pushing down the last remnants of buildings. The crushed and mangled bridges, the ten-foot trenches running down Main Street, the pile of stones that was once an elementary school hardly seem real from half a world away. But earthquakes are very real. In 1976 nearly 300,000 people lost their lives as a result of earthquakes, with a staggering 240,000 fatalities in China alone. If 240,000 people doesn't carry any meaning for you, think of it as being everybody who attended the last three Super Bowl games.

Scientists are still a long way from being able to exert any sort of control over earthquakes, so this leaves them with only one weapon—forecasting. If we can't stop the quake, we can at least move the people. But forecasting means we have to know, with a high degree of accuracy, when and where an earthquake will strike and then issue a warning at least several hours in advance. You can hardly evacuate a city the size of Los Angeles or Tokyo in a couple of minutes. Furthermore, you can't yell, "Earthquake!" on a hunch, move several million people to safer ground—provided you know where safer ground is going to be—and then say, "Oh, gee, sorry. I guess there's no quake after all." It is, indeed, a tall order to be an accurate forecaster, and so far not even the self-proclaimed clairvoyants, gypsies, and psychics are all that good.

Ah . . . but the animals are.

There is a man in California who reads the Lost and Found section of the local papers every day without fail. No, he is not looking for his missing schnauzer. He is not, in fact, looking for any one particular animal. Instead, the man is faithfully keeping a running total of all the pets reported missing in a twenty-four-hour period. Sound boring? Not for long. Sooner than you might think, the number of losts will shoot up dramatically, and that's when the man gets on the phone to the geologists. "Earthquake on the way," he tells them. "The number of losts just doubled."

The man's theory is simple. Animals are able to sense the subtle clues given off by the ground, the rocks, and even the planet's magnetic field just prior to an earthquake, and they react in panic. Birds may screech and fly in circles, horses may stamp the ground, cows may low, and the family cocker spaniel may up and run away.

Weird? Well, maybe not. Consider this:

Concépcion, Chile, 1835

It is 10:30 A.M., and the sky is filled with shrieking seabirds. They fly insanely above the trees, swooping and rising in great loops that circle and circle back again.

11:30 A.M. Horses begin to stomp the ground uneasily, their tails swishing, their withers and flanks quivering as if to chase away flies. But there are no flies. There are no insects at all.

If the townspeople notice the unusually restless behavior, they think little of it. They are busy with their own affairs. Mothers nurse their young. Children chase each other through the streets, laughing and playing at games that have no name. Workers in the fields bend to their tasks, their shirts soaked with sweat, their foreheads glistening. Women grind corn into meal and patiently prepare salsas spiced hot with chili peppers. And Concépcion counts the minutes.

11:39. The animals have scattered, driven by their knowledge of the impending danger.

11:40. The quake strikes, and Concépcion falls like a city made of cards.

The story of the animals of Concépcion is hardly an isolated case. In fact, it is just one in a long list of fantastic earthquake tales dating as far back as three thousand years.

From Japan and China come very early accounts of catfish literally leaping out of the water prior to quakes. (Curiously enough, Japanese legend says that earthquakes are caused by a giant catfish that lives in the mud under the earth.) The ancient Greeks also identified a number of early warning signs: the frenzied flight of birds, an apparent panic among cattle and fowl, and the howling of dogs.

Much more recently, a man in San Francisco noticed some very odd behavior among his pet bullfrogs two days before a modest quake struck the Bay Area. On Sunday, according to the man, the adult frogs had begun to hop about much more than usual. By Monday, the young frogs were croaking loudly and swimming around their aquarium in clockwise circles. The croaking is especially interesting because young frogs do not croak. Only adult males do and then only during the mating season.

On Tuesday the quake struck. Although it measured only 4.7,* the frogs had apparently sensed it coming.

It was hard to miss the panic among the animals in the Skopje, Yugoslavia, zoo in 1963, only nobody saw it for what it was. Long before daybreak, the zookeepers were awakened by a terrific din. It sounded (even though they knew it was impossible) as if a herd of wild and snorting elephants were running rampant through the grounds. Not a little dismayed by the unusual noise, the zookeepers crept somewhat warily from their beds and went to

---

*The Richter Scale (named for Charles Richter) is a kind of "strength scale" used to measure earthquakes. The lower the Richter number, the less severe the quake. Quakes above 6.0 are very destructive, and anything above 8.0 is considered a great earthquake. Quakes that register 8.0 occur once every five to ten years.

investigate. What they found was a herd of wild and snorting elephants stampeding (as best they could) inside their cages. Great clouds of dust had begun to rise from the floors of the cages as the elephants stamped and bellowed and wailed their distress in the not-so-still-anymore night air. And then, as if to add insult to injury, the lions and tigers joined in, pacing and roaring as only big cats know how to do.

Meanwhile, over at police headquarters, the law had its hands full with two howling bloodhounds. The dogs refused to be calmed and were trying to scramble away through an open window.

Clearly, all the signs were there. Yugoslavia is earthquake prone, lying in the wide band that runs through southern Europe and across into Asia. The animals were more than a little agitated; they were downright hysterical. But no one acted, and before the sun rose, the peaceful, almost lazy town of Skopje, Yugoslavia, was completely destroyed by one of the worst earthquakes in its history. It measured 6.0 on the Richter scale and took eleven hundred lives.

From Seattle, Washington, comes another zoo tale about the frenzied activity that occurred on March 27, 1964. The animals had suddenly begun howling, croaking, screeching, snorting, roaring, bellowing, and in general kicking up quite a fuss. Earthquake on the way? Well, yes and no. No for Seattle, yes for Alaska, and not a small one, either. This turned out to be the great Alaskan quake of 1964, hitting an astonishing 8.5! The quake was so powerful, it was estimated to have released two hundred thousand megatons of energy, which is four hundred times greater than the total energy released by all the atomic bombs ever exploded. Alaska was ripped open. No wonder the animals a thousand miles away sensed it coming!

Closer to home but hardly noticed was the curious activity of several Alaskan Kodiak bears that emerged from their winter sleep two weeks early and headed for parts unknown. If this unusual wake-up response was a direct result of the impending quake, it is quite impressive. Whatever it was that the bears felt or heard or smelled was apparently detectable at least fourteen days in advance of the strike. This in itself should give us food for thought.

Animals may be much better attuned to the subtle changes that constantly occur in and on our planet. They may be able to pick up on smells, sounds, fluctuations in the magnetic field, and even increased levels of argon and other gases. Everyone knows that nocturnal animals such as the raccoon and cat have much keener night sight than we do. Bats are famous for their extraordinary hearing, and fish are being shown to have an extreme sensitivity to submarine vibrations.

Until very recently, it was really only the Chinese who took animals seriously as possible earthquake predictors. This is not to say that they totally have abandoned their tiltmeters and creep meters* and other high-tech hardware, but they have definitely been giving dogs, donkeys, and pandas their due.

After two severe earthquakes rocked China in 1966, then-Premier Chou En-lai formally declared "the people's war on earthquakes." Huge amounts of money and resources went into earthquake research in an effort to learn more about why quakes occur, where and how often they are likely to strike, and most important, how to forecast them. In less than eight years, the government had set up seventeen observatories and over two hundred regional seismic stations in China. Indeed, this was war.

But perhaps the most extraordinary part was the manual. It was published by the seismological office in Tientsin and distributed to as many of China's 800 million people as possible. Illustrated in full color, the manual listed the various kinds of strange behavior seen in animals prior to earthquakes and urged people to keep an eye out for these precursors:

Cattle, sheep, horses, and mules do not enter corrals;
Rats move their homes and flee;
Hibernating snakes leave their burrows early; and
Frightened pigeons fly continuously
and do not return to their nests.

*Tiltmeters, as their name suggests, measure the tilting of the earth's surface. Creep meters measure the amount of creep or movement along a fault line.

Well, all this seemed about as scientific as forecasting the weather with a pack of tarot cards, but the Chinese were dead serious. And as things turned out, the seismographs and other equipment only assisted in forecasting what became the great quake of 1975; it was the animals that really saved the day.

It began in 1970, four years after the premier had declared earthquake war. Scientists in Liaoning Province in Manchuria had recorded a series of significant ground shocks and immediately issued a long-range warning. In seismologist talk, what this means is that an earthquake is expected sometime in the future. Hardly impressive. In China, as in California, you can say that any day of the week without the benefit of fancy machinery. In any event, the scientists wanted it known that something big was on the way.

During the early part of 1974, the number of small tremors increased fivefold, and again the seismologists issued a prediction. A significant earthquake would strike the region within two years.

December. More tremors, one of which registered a 4.8. The scientists refined their prediction. The earthquake would strike within the next six months and measure at least 5.5 on the Richter scale.

The people tensed but they did not move. Like the Californians, the Chinese had developed nerves of steel.

February 1975. Liaoning Province is shivering in the cold of a hard winter. The temperature has dropped below freezing, and long icicles hang like daggers from roofs and doorways. The ground continues to shake as if it, too, is shivering in the frozen air. But the nerves of steel begin to bend because now the animals are involved.

One after the other, the reports pour into the seismological office, like pages torn from the people's earthquake manual. Snakes have been seen rousing themselves from hibernation* and crawling out onto the frozen ground where, because they are unable to regulate their body temperature, they face certain death. Rats are dashing brazenly through the streets to the horror and disgust of the citizens. Pigs, hardly known for their agility, are climbing walls, squealing excitedly, and actually biting off each other's tails. Geese have begun flying in ever-ascending and then descending circles across the land like living tornadoes.

February 4. A Tuesday. Early morning and the animal activity is at a feverish pitch. The geese are screaming, rising into the air in frenzied loops and circles high above the city of Haicheng. Horses are kicking excitedly at their stalls, whinnying and baring their great yellow teeth. Cows, not yet released to pasture, strain to get out. Something is wrong. It is in the air, perhaps, or carried on the wind. It is a smell, maybe, or a humming deep underground. The earth looks the same, but it is not the same, and the animals know it.

*To fully appreciate this, see the next chapter, "The Big Sleep." For an animal to rouse itself from hibernation, it is either in grave physical distress or something is threatening it.

The sun climbs. The animals wail. The ground quivers in geologic spasms rising to a severe shock that pushes the Richter to 4.8. Then all is quiet—eerily, creepy-crawly quiet. The planet hangs poised. . . .

It's 2 P.M. local time, and the officials have seen enough. The land is silent. The animals have all gone. The message is clear.

"Citizens of Haicheng!" cry the radios. "We require all people to leave their homes. There will probably be a major earthquake tonight. We repeat: Leave your homes immediately!"

From their shops and businesses, their schools and houses, the people of Liaoning Province pour, clutching a few belongings. They are curiously calm. Temporary shelters have been set up in parks and other open areas, and volunteers point the way. Quickly and efficiently, the hospitals are evacuated, and livestock are led to safer quarters. In less than five hours, well over a million people respond to the urgent radio message, broadcast, the scientists will later admit, because a bunch of animals had grown restless.

7:36 P.M. The earthquake strikes.

It is now appropriate to ask, how do the animals do it?

While the Chinese and Russians have been studying the phenomenon for quite some time, Western scientists have just started to take animal prognostication seriously. At first, though, anyone who even hinted that he or she was involved in this kind of research was likely to be laughed right out of the seismological office. Now, however, even the biggest doubters have had their scientific interest piqued.

In the early 1970s, Dr. Ruth Simon, a respected geophysicist and biologist with the U.S. Geological Survey and the Colorado School of Mines, began experimenting with cockroaches. Dr. Simon admits that she can't stand the creepy little things, but points out that cockroaches are perfect subjects. Their dot-size brain and very simple nervous system allow for little more than basic "gut" reactions. Unlike the higher animals, cockroaches don't fuss about the kind of food they are being served (they eat absolutely anything), or the weather, or their sleeping arrangements. (They often sleep in your walls.) Instead—and this is one of the reasons why they have survived since the time of the dinosaurs—cockroaches simply respond to changes in their environment. Period. So they were just what the doctor ordered to star in her earthquake prediction experiments.

Simon built a few fancy cockroach condominiums, complete with air-conditioning and a well-stocked larder and then wired them with delicate sensors that would pick up the slightest cockroach movement. After she bugged the bughouse, Dr. Simon moved in a handful of her wriggily tenants and transported the condos to a nice little plot of land on the San Andreas Fault. The San Andreas Fault shifts so often, Dr. Simon did not have to wait long before she started getting data from the seismic stations. She then compared the seismometers' printouts to the cockroach activity printouts and found two very remarkable things. First, about thirty-six hours prior to either a tremor or a "storm," the cockroaches became unusually active. Did they sense anything? And if so, what? More important, with what did they sense it? Do cockroaches have an as-yet-undiscovered receptor—an earthquake-detecting nose or eardrum or hair follicle?

Second—and this is really curious—during the tremors, the cockroaches were very, very quiet. This is exactly the opposite of what you might expect. Were they too frightened or shocked to move? Or were they *unable* to move?

The results of Dr. Simon's studies have yet to be determined, but they certainly have given us something to think about. Probably the most intriguing part is the simplicity of the kind of animal sensing the earthquakes. A cockroach is nowhere near as complicated as a human being, and yet, it is catching the subtle clues that we apparently are missing. Animal amazing, indeed.

While Dr. Simon works with her nasty little subjects along the San Andreas Fault, the scientists in Japan are busy with catfish. It has been known for a while that birds and bees are highly sensitive to all kinds of subtle geologic changes. Homing pigeons, for example, can detect small fluctuations in the earth's magnetic field, and this helps them find their way around. A bee's famous "waggle dance" is really an elaborate map to the honey source based on magnetic-field and light clues. But fish, too, have been shown to be members of the "sensitivity society." Fish have something called a lateral line system running down their flanks, which can pick up low-frequency vibrations and changes in the movement of the water in which they are submerged. It is a kind of early warning system telling the fish that something is in the vicinity. (Fish are not exactly famous for their eyesight.) Some kinds of fish have even developed voltage detectors. All creatures are surrounded by a faint bioelectric field, and sharks in particular are so good at sensing this, they can zoom in on a flounder that has completely buried itself in the sand.

The Japanese scientists hope to be able to use this fishy hypersensitivity to one day predict earthquakes and save lives. And who knows? Maybe we will see a time when every home in earthquake country comes equipped with a pool of catfish in the backyard. The insurance companies might even consider giving homeowner's discounts if you own a fish tank. Or a dog. Or a gerbil. Who says seismometers have to be made out of metal? The best earthquake device ever invented might be clawing your furniture.

CHAPTER 2

The Big Sleep

H ere's the scene:
We are several million miles from earth, hurtling through the cosmos in the spaceship *Discovery* from the movie *2001: A Space Odyssey*. Our course has been preset and is being maintained by the sophisticated HAL 9000 computer. On one of the ship's levels a small group of astronauts lies nearly frozen inside gleaming white cocoons. A small, rectangular faceplate, sprinkled with ice crystals, reveals peaceful faces covered with the thinnest layer of frost. The astronauts are in cold sleep, their bodies chilled to just above thirty-two degrees Fahrenheit. Their breathing and heart rate have been slowed by perhaps 90 percent. They neither take in food nor eliminate waste products. They do not dream. They will pass

almost the entire voyage in this extraordinary state, hardly aging, deep in hibernation.

In the film it all looked so real, so possible. Surely the medical team at NASA would be able to imitate Stanley Kubrick's sleep trick when the star ships were completed. They'd inject some kind of antifreeze, wouldn't they, into the astronauts' veins? They'd put the astronauts into slumber sacks or sleep pods and then slowly lower their temperature. After all, that's how Arthur C. Clarke and Stanley Kubrick did it on the movie set. And they weren't even doctors.

We bought it all, and we believed, in story after science-fiction story. But the secret of hibernation remains as elusive as ever, still one of nature's very greatest mysteries. Only a small handful of animals can put themselves into this most amazing of sleep states—the ground squirrel, woodchuck (groundhog), chipmunk, some bats, and a few others are considered true hibernators. Bears and raccoons are just deep sleepers and can be aroused very easily. A poke or gentle prod will do it. (Not advisable, though. Bears are apt to be a bit cranky when they are awakened.) But when the ground squirrel sacks out, it's really out. It's so out, in fact, that you can pick it up, roll it around, and even perform surgery on it! When a ground squirrel goes into hibernation, it is truly nature at its amazing best.

No matter where they are—and scientists have put them in some pretty strange environments—ground squirrels always know when the time for hibernation is at hand, but this has almost nothing to do with either the outside temperature or the season. Ground squirrels operate on their own time, a time governed by a mysterious biological clock that suddenly "goes off" somewhere inside the animals.

Scientists theorize that each of us has a biological clock that is keyed to the cycles of daylight and darkness. Even with the invention of electric lights, we still continue to sleep during the hours of darkness. This may be because we are just not adapted to night prowling. Our eyesight is lousy at night and compared to other animals, such as bats, we are all but deaf. So we sleep. While there *are* people who work through the deep night hours—newspaper reporters and police on the "graveyard shift"— their bodies never quite make the adjustment, and they always feel a little out of sync with the rest of the world.

But a day/night cycle would hardly be useful to a hibernating animal. Hibernators sleep for six months or more at a time, and when they finally awaken, they could care less if the sun is shining or the moon is up. There is an astronomical cycle that does affect the hibernator, though. It is the small, almost imperceptible change in the length of the day as governed by the earth's movement around the sun.

As winter approaches, the days grow shorter and shorter, the hours of daylight, fewer. While the difference each day is only minutes, perhaps the ground squirrel's biological clock is so precisely set it is able to detect the change. Then, at the right time, the squirrel's bio alarm goes off, and the animal automatically enters the hibernation mode.

The ground squirrel hibernates for an astonishing eight months of the year and during this time he will eat absolutely nothing, so his first order of business before he nods off is to fatten himself up. (Chipmunks cheat. They stash food under their beds and wake up every so often to grab a little midwinter snack.) When the ground squirrel is at last ready to put himself into cold storage, he has doubled his weight, although this may be not as phenomenal as it sounds. A ground squirrel might be only about the size of a chipmunk to begin with, so two times very little is still very little. But the statistic becomes impressive when you realize that the ground squirrel has to make his extra fat last him for eight months.* Slowly and with extreme efficiency, he feeds off his store of fat using the barest minimum needed to maintain his life functions.

When the ground squirrel reaches his target top weight, he digs himself a little burrow three feet underground where the temperature is constant regardless of what is going on topside. Then, in he goes, guided by the same mysterious bio clock, and literally rolls himself up into a ball. He does this to conserve body heat. When

---

*In the same period of time, the average American consumes in excess of two hundred eighty pounds of vegetables, fruit, and beef, and about one hundred ninety eggs. Furthermore, every day we scoff up thirty-four hundred calories (dieters excluded), an amount that the ground squirrel could probably make last well into the following year.

hibernating, his head and front legs are tucked down into his belly, and his hind legs seem almost to have disappeared into his haunches. The only thing sticking out is his tiny tail.

Chill down takes a couple of hours, probably to give the squirrel's body time to adjust to what will be a huge drop in temperature. Normally, the ground squirrel's body temperature is about 95 degrees. During hibernation it falls to somewhere in the 35-degree range—a 60-degree drop! This particular little feat has got the scientists shaking their heads in absolute amazement. If we, starting at 98.6, could lower our body temperature by even half that of the ground squirrel—30 degrees—our heart would stop dead, which explains why we have not yet been able to put anybody into hibernation.

At thirty-five degrees, the ground squirrel's heartbeat has dropped from three hundred beats per minute to just five. Respiration is now a mere one breath every several minutes. The ground squirrel is in the deepest of all sleeps, tucked up in a mysterious realm where scientists have not even been able to measure brain activity. (An EEG fails to record much of anything when the squirrel's body temperature drops below seventy-seven degrees.)

The ground squirrel seems to be at the mercy of his own hibernation, but he is not. He apparently has a few fail-safe systems that automatically go into operation when needed. First, every now and then the squirrel rouses himself and takes a few deep breaths. Scientists think this oxygenates the squirrel's body and prevents the buildup of deadly carbon dioxide. The squirrel's lungs work like bellows, in and out, in and out, aerating the squirrel's tiny body and ridding it of toxic waste products. Then, his yoga exercises completed, the squirrel recurls himself and plunges once again into his strange sleep.

A kind of internal thermostat provides the squirrel with his second fail-safe system. Scientists know virtually nothing about this strange mechanism, but they are convinced that it lies somewhere in a small area of the squirrel's brain called the hypothalamus. The hypothalamus is believed to be the body's great regulator, controlling such vital systems as sweating, shivering, and sleep. So if for any reason the squirrel's body temperature falls to the freezing point, the hypothalamic thermostat kicks in and immediately rouses the squirrel. Like a watchful guard on sentry duty, the hypothalamus somehow keeps the squirrel's internal temperature precisely regulated. Thus the squirrel is protected against death by the very activity designed to increase his chances of survival. Truly, it is a beautiful system.

The ground squirrel emerges from hibernation as slowly and methodically as he entered. Gradually, his heart begins to quicken, sending an ever-increasing flow of blood to organs and muscles. Then the squirrel's body temperature inches upward, warming the heart, brain, and lungs, upon which all the other organs depend. The squirrel unfolds in stages as he comes out. First he is a fur ball, but a while later we find him lying motionless on his stomach. He turns over and for a time remains on his back. If you watch closely, you can see his tiny chest rising and falling as he takes deeper and more frequent breaths. The next position is on his side with his legs outstretched, and finally he begins to awaken in earnest and sit up.

Initially, his legs are folded beneath him, and he is hunched down in what looks like an "on your mark" position. Soon, however, the squirrel's waking equilibrium returns, and the squirrel is standing upright, all bright eyed and bushy tailed.

The ground squirrel's emergence from hibernation is one of the most captivating sights in nature, and you can't help feeling just a little jealous. Not only can this tiny mammal do something we can't, but he makes it look ridiculously easy.

For the ground squirrels, the bats, the woodchucks, and a handful of others who have mastered the technique, hibernation is a safe way of getting through the winter. It also extends the creature's life span by slowing down metabolism and all life functions. So it is no wonder that hibernation caught the fancy of science-fiction writers. But as usual, the laboratory scientists are having a little trouble catching up. Jules Verne had us on the moon a century before NASA managed it, and the pages of *Astounding Science Fiction* showed us ray guns and disintegrators long before the laser made its appearance. Why are the writers so much smarter than the scientists?

Well, they're not, really. It just seems that way because the writers aren't stuck with the task of figuring out how to make their ideas work. So it wasn't until very recently that biologists were finally able to start probing the mysteries of hibernation with any degree of confidence.

In the late 1960s, biologists attempted an extraordinary experiment. They withdrew blood from hibernating ground squirrels and injected it into ground squirrels that were not hibernating. (The nonhibernating squirrels were kept awake under controlled laboratory conditions.) Amazingly, within forty-eight hours, the active squirrels went into hibernation.

The following year, the experimenters withdrew blood from hibernating woodchucks and injected it into nonhibernating ground squirrels. Once again, the active animals went into hibernation.

Scientists think there is a hibernation trigger in the blood of hibernating animals. The trigger substance, they say, builds up gradually, and when it reaches a certain level, the animal cannot help but go into hibernation. The scientists also found that the substance apparently doesn't make distinctions between animals since ground squirrels were sent into hibernation by the blood from woodchucks.

But it gets better.

A number of years after the ground squirrel/woodchuck experiments, the blood from hibernating ground squirrels was injected into rhesus monkeys, and rhesus monkeys *do not hibernate at all!* The results were startling, to say the least. Within a very short period of time, the monkeys became sluggish and sleepy. Their body temperature dropped, their breathing and pulse rate slowed, and for several days they ate almost nothing. Hibernation? No, but certainly something tantalizingly close to it.

Scientists admit they do not know the nature of this mysterious hibernation blood trigger, but it will likely be just a matter of time before the biochemists sort it all out. And then . . . ?

HELP WANTED: FIVE ASTRONAUTS TO ENTER HIBERNATION FOR THREE HUNDRED YEARS AND TRAVEL ACROSS GALAXY. GOOD PAY. ROOM AND BOARD INCLUDED. GROWTH OPPORTUNITY. REPLY CAPTAIN FOSDICK T. BRAVEHEART, BOX 2, WASHINGTON, DC.

Welcome to the real 2001.

CHAPTER 3

The Body Shop

It often comes as something of a shock to be told by your biology teacher to "gently make three horizontal slices" in the living, breathing animal waiting patiently on your lab tray. Even the toughest shrink back. For several minutes, the air in the classroom is heavy with 1) loathing for the teacher, 2) self-disgust at the murderous act you are about to commit, and 3) cowardice in technicolor. Scalpels hang poised. Throats gulp. And then almost in unison, the entire class gently makes three horizontal slices.

The recipient of such treatment is a small, cross-eyed flatworm called a planarian, a staple of school biology labs. Despite the drastic surgery, however, it never appears to be the least bit bothered and, most significantly, goes right on living just as it did before you and your band of mercenaries showed up. Curious, indeed.

If you have a conscience, you think about your little planarian all through the week, wondering how it is faring and if its severed head misses its body, its body misses its tail, and its tail misses everything that once grew above it. The planarian, though, is busy with far more important matters than musing over some stranger. Like a handful of others in its animal-amazing fraternity, it is working on a reconstruction project the likes of which the greatest scientific minds in the world cannot duplicate. In a few days, you will see the dramatic results.

At the appointed time, the students retrieve their respective planarian trays, but even before they have returned to their lab tables, they can see that an apparent miracle of zoology has occurred. On each tray, there are now three fully formed planaria, all of which bear a striking family resemblance to the original model. What has happened in the course of a couple of weeks?

With remarkable exactitude, the individual pieces of planarian have regenerated themselves: The head has regrown a body and tail, the body has fashioned itself a head and tail, and the tail has supplied its missing head and body. If students are not allowed to peek at the intermediate stages of the process, the planarian's regeneration feat is shocking, but it becomes positively fascinating when you watch this simple animal slowly but surely making itself whole again—or rather, making its three selves whole again. Even better than that, however is the fact that this regenerative power is the planarian's secret, a mysterious gift from nature that science has yet to understand.

Regeneration is an ability given in varying degrees to few members of the animal world. Salamanders, for example, can grow a new tail, but their tail cannot grow a new body. Lobsters can manage claws, but claws cannot make new lobsters. The starfish, though, runs a complete body shop and can grow a whole new self from just an arm, a feat that Maine oystermen (and women) are not too crazy about.

Starfish love oysters and can devastate an oyster bed in a very short period of time. Now, since oysters are decidedly quite delicious to eat and starfish are not, the oystermen are out gunning for starfish.

One of the rangers at Acadia National Park in Maine tells the story of an irate (and not too clever) oysterman who, fed up and disgusted with the whole starfish business, hauled in a big bunch of the spiny little things and proceded to chop them into tiny pieces. "That'll teach ya!" he screamed, and hurled the pieces back into the sea. But each piece did what came naturally, and in very short order the starfish were back in greater numbers than ever before. The oysterman, one can only hope, has figured out the error of his ways.

Limb regeneration always has fascinated us, and we have watched in awe as salamanders slowly but surely grow their tails back and planarians replace their heads. Even more astonishing are the reports of a human baby's ability to regrow the tips of its fingers! This was seen, not once, but several times at the Children's Hospital in Sheffield, England. According to Dr. Cynthia Ellingsworth, the severed finger, dressed but otherwise untreated, regenerates in about three months on the average. And all the details are there—fingernail, sensation, even the loops and whorls of the original fingerprint!

But it is really in the lower animals—the newts and salamanders, the lizards and starfish, and of course, the planarian—that we see regeneration at its most impressive. These are creatures that can repair themselves after severe physical trauma. How do they do it? And why are there so few regeneration magicians in the animal world? And why, perhaps most of all, can't we do it? After age ten even fingertip regeneration is lost to us, and about all we can manage is limited bone and skin regrowth. What does the salamander have that a human being doesn't have?

You might at first think that the salamander can regenerate its limbs because it has *less* than we do. It's a simple animal, not nearly as complicated, and the blueprint for a new limb is probably equivalent to, say, a crayon drawing. Easy stuff. But scientists have found that the so-called "lower" animals are just as complex as we are. A leg is a leg. Period. It doesn't seem to matter to nature that some legs are smaller than others, covered with scaly green skin, or end in funny-looking toes. The basic structure, the thing that becomes *leg*, has the same basic design whether you are a frog, a zebra, or even Bigfoot. So, okay. All legs are created equal, but surely there must be *some* difference between salamanders and human beings.

Interestingly enough, scientists already had part of the answer as far back as the eighteenth century; they just didn't know it. They had discovered that when an animal suffers an injury, the wound immediately begins to generate a positive electrical charge. Furthermore, the greater the injury, the higher the voltage. But this was only a piece of the puzzle, so it didn't look like much to the scientists, and they filed it away for use later on— much later on as it turned out.

It wasn't until the mid 1950s that an anatomy professor studying regeneration in animals hit on this little gem: When an animal that cannot regenerate loses a limb, the electrical charge emitted by the stump grows slowly weaker and weaker as scar tissue is formed. When the stump scars over completely, the electrical charge shuts down for good. But if the animal can regrow its lost limb, then scar tissue *doesn't* form. The stump doesn't seal itself off but instead begins to regenerate new bone, muscle, tissue, and nerves—and that is the difference between salamanders and people. Our body forms scar tissue.

Furthermore, in a stump that is regenerating, not only does the electrical voltage remain as strong as ever, the charge flips from positive to negative. Like a fabulous craftsman, the animal fashions a new leg with painstaking accuracy. Every detail is there, right down to the tiniest, most seemingly insignificant skin fold, a precise duplicate of the original. When the regeneration process is at last complete, the electrical charge fades to nothing, presumably because there is no longer any wound.

Well, now. What have we here? Electricity as the great healer? It seems extraordinary. But in the 1800s, charlatans peddled all kinds of doodads and gizmos that plugged in and supposedly cured people of everything short of bubonic plague—and maybe even that, too. There were electricity chairs to sit in, hats and bizarre-looking electrical tiaras. There was even a washtublike device touted by its manufacturer to cure gout and rheumatism.

As you might expect, the scientific community thought all this electricity business was a pack of laughs, but that was then and this is now, and nobody's laughing anymore. In the 1970s, Dr. Steven Smith, working out of the University of Kentucky, performed a dramatic experiment that dethroned Godzilla as the most famous amphibian. Smith amputated the right foreleg of a frog—an animal that doesn't handle regeneration any better than we do—and implanted a tiny battery and an electrode leading to the end of the stump. The battery gave off a continuous negative charge similar, Smith hoped, to the negative electrical current that is present in regenerating limbs. While the results were truly eye-popping, they did not occur overnight. The entire process took about a year, but yes, indeed, the frog actually regrew its entire leg—toes and all!

How did the frog's stump know what to make? How did it know that it had to refashion so much bone, so much muscle, nerves of such and such a length, green skin, and four skinny toes?

To find the answer we have to go back to the womb. All of us, as you probably know, begin life as a single fertilized cell. Almost at once, the cell begins dividing—two, four, eight, sixteen, thirty-two—in a geometric progression that quickly becomes a little ball of cells called a blastula. The word blastula is from the Greek *blastos* meaning "bud," and indeed, that's exactly what it is. Like a tiny bud on a branch, the blastula soon will bloom into all the details that make a living organism: heart, lungs, muscles, bone, arms, legs, fingernails, even individual hair shafts. The instructions for each organ, each feature, is contained in the long, twisted strands of DNA in the cells that make up the blastula. The blastula is then the original body shop where all the parts are made.

But the body shop does not remain in operation for very long. Nearly every animal quickly loses the mysterious ability to make limbs and organs as the cells of the blastula did in the earliest days of life. Yes, we can manage skin. We can regrow some bone and a little bit of muscle, but once severed, the body part is gone forever.

Only in the cells of the blastula lies the secret of regeneration.

Except . . .

Newts and salamanders, starfish and planarians can create a sort of makeshift blastula at the site of the amputation. It is a bundle of cells that scientists call a blastema. The blastema *somehow* knows just what is missing and how to make it. A salamander that loses its toes produces a blastema that makes toes—not a leg or another foot, only toes, only what has been lost. Truly, it is a remarkable process.

Over the years, scientists have learned a great deal about regeneration, but the closer we look, the more blurred the picture seems to get. For example, animals that regenerate do not get cancer. The lizard can regenerate its tail but nothing else. If cancer cells are implanted into the lizard's body, the cancer flourishes; if they are implanted into its tail, the cancer vanishes.

Hormones appear to play some role in regeneration. When a lizard's adrenal gland is removed, the animal loses its ability to regenerate its tail. However, if a hormone called prolactin is injected into the lizard, the ability returns. Even more fascinating, prolactin is found in the pituitary gland, and one of the jobs of the pituitary gland is to regulate growth!

The plot does indeed thicken.

There will come, no doubt, a brave new world in which we are able to regenerate bits and pieces of ourselves as easily as the starfish and the planarian. The artificial limbs and hearts, the hearing aids and implants will no longer have to be shipped in from the body shop.

The body shop will be us.

CHAPTER 4

United We Think

A cadia National Park in Maine, sometime in midsummer:

You have come to the end of the trail. The rest is thick forest and a slippery, rocky terrain that slopes sharply uphill. As usual, it rained the night before, and you know from experience that the ground beneath the brown pine-needle cover will be a slick goo. You swat at a mosquito and think of the hoards endlessly breeding in the heavy humidity of the forest. No, you decide, pulling off your shoes and socks. You will stay right here, alongside a lake whose name only the locals know.

You scramble down the embankment and splash into water that is surprisingly warm. Smilingly contentedly, the water lapping against your rolled-up jeans, you wade past a narrow strip of smooth rocks near the shore and out to where the floor becomes a kind of squishy mud-sand. Sunlight pierces the lake, making the water golden. The lake is very clear, and as you peer into the shallow depths you find yourself standing smack in the middle of a rather large school of fish. The fish are almost the same color as the mud, so whenever they swim too far away you lose sight of them. Mesmerized, almost, by their graceful movements, you begin to follow them. From somewhere beyond the rocks a loon calls, low and mournful, but all else is silence.

The fish dart back and forth through the yellow water, first to the right, then to the left, then to the right again. They all turn together, each individual somehow know-ing, or perhaps anticipating, what the group is going to do. There are no stragglers, no fish on the edges of the group that don't get the message to turn. There must be sixty or seventy fish, and they move in a tight unit, casting a dark shadow, like a cloud, on the soft, sandy bottom. And you begin to wonder, How are they doing it? How do these mindless little fish know when to turn? Who is the conductor, the lead pilot who says, "Okay, guys. To the left on three. One . . . two. . . ." Gradually it begins to dawn on you, as it does on almost anyone who takes the time to really watch a school of fish, that something grandly mysterious is happening.

Seventy separate individuals that cannot communi-cate with each other are acting as if they are a single organism. A school marching band of seventy tenth-graders could not do this. Professional dancers in the corps of the American Ballet Theatre could not do this without hours of rehearsal. But here is a bunch of fish, no bigger than the sardines you find in a tin in the grocery store, executing precise movements with lightning speed at virtually the exact same time.

Animal amazing, indeed.

Birds, of course, do this sort of thing all the time, and on almost any given day of the year you can see geese sailing overhead in their spectacular V formations and stirring up our wanderlust for faraway lands. In 1813, John Audubon saw, according to his notes, some 300 million passenger pigeons *an hour* pass overhead, obscuring the sun "like an eclipse." The phenomenon continued for several days as the flock, which finally numbered several *billion* individuals, swept through the skies of Wisconsin and beyond. Today, not one passenger pigeon remains, and the species has been declared extinct, but group flight—the mass movement of thousands upon thousands of birds—still continues.

At the edge of Africa's famous and magnificent Kalahari Desert, red-billed quelas come to breed, and come by the millions. Thousands of nests fill each tree over an area of some six square miles. Ordered by nature's clock, all the little quelas hatch at the same time, and a few weeks later, every single bird in every single colony takes to the air. They rise en masse, like a great brown dust storm, celebrating the special kind of freedom that only birds can know.

Together, the quelas swoop and glide, rising and falling as if they were one. Together they touch down to feed, and together they take to the air again. The speed with which they bank and change direction is truly staggering, and yet not a one loses pace or placement. Seemingly it is a group mind that guides the quelas. Or mental telepathy. Or some mysterious means of transmission operating so fast that it races through the flock of millions of birds in an eye blink. You have to wonder how quickly a thousand human beings could relay the message to turn right, one person at a time. . . .

University of Rhode Island scientists have measured the reaction time of starlings to learn how fast it takes them to respond to a stimulus such as a slight bump or a nudge. The results: a mere 30 milliseconds—1/300th of a second—considerably faster than an eye blink. But if the birds and fish are getting some kind of cue, as the experiments seem to suggest, who sends the original message? Which bird selects the flight path and then passes the information on to the flock?

At the University of Washington, Wayne Potts spent many hours filming birds in flight and discovered that it is a single bird at the very edge of the flock that starts a maneuver. The rest of the birds—all one hundred, one thousand, or one million of them—follow suit. The clue appears to be a slight shift in position, which is first detected by the bird nearest the leader. Reaction time: sixty-two milliseconds. Bird number three then gets its cue from bird number two, but its reaction time is faster.

Bird number four reacts still faster, and so on, until by the time the cue has been passed through the entire flock to the last remaining bird, the reaction time is down to an astonishing fifteen milliseconds. Scientists call this phenomenon a maneuver wave, something that you may have helped to create while watching a baseball or football game at the stadium, although sports fans are a lot slower than birds.

But maneuver waves do not explain the oceangoing marvel that is the Portuguese man-of-war. Like a ghostly sailing ship from a Jules Verne novel, the Portuguese man-of-war haunts the world's subtropical oceans. Its pink, gas-filled float can measure more than a foot from end to end. A ridged crest, like a sail, tops the float to allow the creature a curious maneuverability. Beneath hangs a snarl of long, crimped tentacles, extending forty feet down, where they gently sway with the rhythm of the bottom currents. The tentacles are fishing lines, but they are something else, too. Each one contains yet another tentacle, dark blue in color and bearing a small cluster of stinging cells. The softest brush with a Portuguese man-of-war's tentacles is enough to activate the cells, and to all but two kinds of marine animal, paralysis is immediate. Indeed, the Portuguese man-of-war is silent and deadly, lazily cruising where it pleases, like a living mine field.

Most people just assume that the Portuguese man-of-war is a jellyfish, but it is not. Technically speaking, it isn't even an animal. It is, instead, a colony of small, weird-looking creatures called polyps. A polyp is not much more than a barrel-shaped body with tentacles sticking out of the top. It does nothing except feed itself, using its tentacles to sweep food into its mouth. The most well-known polyps are those that band together to form the various corals, which also do practically nothing except eat.

If you have ever seen pictures of coral or been lucky enough to encounter it while snorkeling or scuba diving, you know that coral is uniform throughout. A large colony of brain coral looks like a large brain. Star coral endlessly repeats its delicate star pattern. Pipe-organ coral grows tube after tube after tube, giving the appearance of a giant pipe organ. In other words, the individual polyps are all the same.

And then there is the Portuguese man-of-war. Four different kinds of polyps combine to create the "creature," which looks to all like a single animal. Each polyp type does only its own job and nothing else. The fishing polyps, for example, catch food, but they are unable to feed themselves. They survive because the entire thing that is the Portuguese man-of-war survives. The polyps that have organized themselves into the float are separate and unique from the two kinds of polyps comprising the tentacles. Indeed, the Portuguese man-of-war is the shape it is not because the DNA of the whole organism is calling the shots as ours does, but because that is how the individual polyps come together.

Now, this would not be impressive if the Portuguese

man-of-war did nothing, if it just drifted hither and yon with the currents. The scientists would not be baffled, and there would be one less subject for this chapter. But the Portuguese man-of-war actually navigates! It trims its sail and tacks down wind. It steers by means of its highly flexible float ridge, which operates like a sail, and the knot of tentacles that have assembled themselves in the aft part of the float so they work like a rudder. Left to the winds of chance, the Portuguese man-of-war would no doubt be tossed around like a cork, but its deliberate actions result in a speed of about four knots when there's a good, stiff breeze.

What are we to make of this? The Portuguese man-of-war is not an animal. It has no brain, no nervous system. It can't think, and yet, when all the parts are added together, this primitive community of individuals acts suspiciously like a single organism as it charts its course over the ocean.

The question has been asked if the Portuguese man-of-war has consciousness. Is it aware of its surroundings? Does it know by external clues when to trim its sail to make efficient use of the wind? And if so, where did this consciousness come from?

The thing we call consciousness is a strange and baffling phenomenon, and scientists admit that they are not at all sure what it is or how it arises. Consider yourself, for example. You are really nothing more than a colony of individual cells. Your cells contain some DNA material, a great deal of water, a nucleus, and some other structures, but no brain. Yet, when billions of these come together in just the right way, the result is a unit—a person—who is indeed conscious. When did this happen? At what point in your development from a single fertilized egg cell did this consciousness arise? Even more mysterious, where did it come from if all the little parts that went into making you were not themselves conscious? While few people are proposing that human beings are built on the same principle as the Portuguese man-of-war, you've got to admit there are some interesting similarities.

Going one step further, we come to the extraordinary theory that suggests there is a grand collective consciousness shared by all members of the same species. That is to say, all laboratory rats, for example, have access to a kind of laboratory rat information source, an evolutionary library that contains everything ever learned by the individual members of the species. The rats are like keyboard operators whose computers are linked to one master computer. In this way, the experiences of a group of rats in a laboratory in Daytona become part of the storehouse of knowledge of all the laboratory rats everywhere. The offspring of the Daytona rats also benefit from the collective consciousness. They are born with a kind of residual memory, a feeling of "having done this thing once before." Although scientists do not have hard proof that such a collective consciousness actually exists, there have been some rather intriguing indications that it *might* exist.

A generation of rats was taught to run a maze to reach a food reward, and the rats' runs were timed. Naturally, as the rats learned the pattern of right and left turns, their times improved. Then the rats were bred and their offspring were placed in the same maze. To almost everyone's astonishment, the young rats took less time than their parents did to learn the maze! It was almost as if they had some vague stored memory about it.

Without an explanation but determined to come up with one, the scientists then bred a second generation of rats and taught their young—the grandchildren of the original students—to run the maze. The results were a little unnerving. The third generation learned the route to the cheese *even faster* than their parents did!

Clearly, something quite remarkable was happening, but what was it? You may suggest that the rats were simply passing along their knowledge of the maze path to their children, but all the evidence thus far suggests that learned information cannot be inherited. What we pass along to our children are physical characteristics and intelligence potential, those pieces of information that are encoded in our genes about the pattern or layout of the organism. So how did the successive generations of laboratory rats get more and more adept at running the maze? Did they tap into a collective consciousness?

An article in the magazine *Science News Letter* in 1946 reported an equally curious situation. Many years ago, the Eagle River in British Columbia, Canada, was home to a wealth of sockeye salmon. Indeed, it provided quite a good income for the local fishermen, so you can well imagine everyone's reaction when the salmon population in the Eagle began to thin out and then all but disappear.

Now salmon, it should be mentioned, are migrators. They are born in rivers, migrate toward the sea, and then return to the river of their birth to spawn (lay their eggs). This is instinct, a strange and powerful force that pushes the salmon on, regardless of the obstacles. The trip upstream is very difficult since the salmon must swim against the flow of rushing water. Many times the salmon have to "jump" churning rapids and cascades, but they always return because the future of the species depends on their arrival at the spawning grounds.

The gradual but steady disappearance of the salmon from the Eagle River puzzled the fishermen, but more than that, they feared for their livelihood. So the people from the local fisheries decided to do something to try to bring the salmon back. Over a period of ten years, they patiently transplanted sockeye salmon eggs from two other rivers. Careful handling and transportation yielded good results . . . up to a point. The salmon eggs hatched quite normally, and just as nature had ordained, the young salmon began their long swim to the sea, where they would grow to adulthood. To keep track of the salmon, the fishermen tagged all the individuals that had hatched from the transplanted eggs, and then they waited. But the months passed and the salmon did not return.

Year after year, the fishermen watched the salmon eggs hatch and the young swim away, never to be seen again. Where they wound up remained forever a mystery, since none of the tagged salmon were found at either of the two rivers from which the eggs had been taken. But certainly the most curious part is how the "eggs" knew not to return to the Eagle River to spawn. Had the parents of the original Eagle population somehow passed this "warning" along to their offspring, who in turn passed it to their offspring, and so on and so on? Did all the sockeye salmon in the area, in perhaps the entire province, know not to return to the Eagle River? Is this sort of intergeneration communication even possible?

Newborn animals seem to be on the receiving end of a whole host of amazing information—actions and even elaborate procedures that they are never taught, never even see! But most amazing of all is the simple fact that the future of the species depends almost entirely on these events unfolding in a very precise manner. One slip, and all the generations yet to come would likely be doomed.

Consider, for instance, the extraordinary case of the spider and the wasp. There are many different kinds of wasps, but the one in our story is a predatory wasp, a wasp that aggressively attacks others for its own gain. Most people think of spiders as being the scoundrels, sneaky nogoodniks who lure innocent insects into their sticky web of death and then paralyze them. This time, though, it's the spider who winds up as the victim.

In scene one, we learn that the wasp is a vegetarian, which is perfectly all right, except that its young are not. Instead, the kids would prefer a nice, muscle-building meat meal. But because the mother wasp adheres strictly to the vegetarian code, she cannot simply wolf down the spider and then regurgitate it for her children. Thus, the stage is set.

Just before the mother wasp is about to give birth, she heads out in search of a spider. This winds up being outrageously easy because the spider of choice has terrible eyesight and even worse hearing, so it neither sees nor hears the wasp sneaking up on it. However, nature in its infinite wisdom has provided the spider with a very acute sense of touch. The barest movement of one of the spider's hairs, and the creature whirls around and chomps down on a careless victim. Now, this would seem to spell the end for the wasp, but it doesn't. For some reason, when the wasp approaches and begins to meander all over the spider's belly, the spider does absolutely nothing. It just sits there, calmly allowing the wasp to poke and probe for the exact spot in which to inject her paralyzing stinger.

When the wasp establishes her bearings and locates the death spot, she climbs down and heads off to dig a little combination birth chamber/spider grave. The spider, meanwhile, waits around like some kind of an idiot. It doesn't run away. It doesn't attack the wasp. It doesn't call in reinforcements. In a little while, the wasp returns, hops back onto the spider, and wriggles herself into position. One, two, three, and the spider has been paralyzed by a creature it had ample opportunity to kill many times over but didn't. Strange, indeed.

Next, the wasp drags the heavy spider to the grave it has dug, stuffs the spider inside, and lashes down its legs. This is just in case the spider suddenly should recover from the wasp's sting and try some funny stuff. Finally, the wasp lays its single egg and affixes it to the side of the spider with a sticky wasp goo. Mom wasp then seals up the grave/birth chamber and heads off for parts unknown, forever ignorant of the outcome of all her efforts.

The outcome, though, is almost always the same.

After the prescribed time, the wasp larva hatches, a little bit of a thing literally surrounded by spider. The spider is obviously too much food for one sitting, but it isn't intended as such. Instead, the spider will last until the young wasp is big and strong enough to venture out on its own.

Now, if the spider were dead, it would quickly begin to rot, and the baby wasp probably would not get past breakfast. But the spider is only paralyzed, and to keep it alive and fresh, the larva begins its feast around the edges, saving the vital, life-sustaining organs for last. It thereby assures itself a good, wholesome meal every time.

Truly, this is one of the great marvels of the animal world, but it is also one of the great mysteries. How do the wasps—both mother and baby—know what to do? Who taught them? As you have seen, the mother wasp doesn't show its baby anything. She's not even around when the little tyke is born. Furthermore, the baby wasp is born knowing not only how to deal with the spider before it comes out of its birth chamber, but also how to "prep" the spider for its own baby.

You might suggest that the entire process did not emerge full blown but was tested and refined and changed gradually through generations of wasps. But think for a minute about the whole scenario. There is no room for a mistake. If the mother wasp misses the vital target spot when she attempts to paralyze the spider, good-bye, wasp. If the baby wasp eats, say, the spider's heart instead of its leg, the spider dies and the wasp starves to death. And what about the spider? It willingly allows itself to be killed! This is hardly in keeping with the spirit of survival. How long is the spider population going to last with this sort of attitude? Are these two creatures tapping into a collective consciousness, or is the entire drama encoded, like a computer program, somewhere in the animals' DNA strands?

Another remarkable thing about the spider and the wasp story is the fact that there is really no room for evolution. The wasp's sting, the consumption of the spider—the whole bit—has to be all or nothing. Floundering and failed attempts, trials and errors, immediately spell death—not for a single wasp, but sooner or later for the entire species! In other words, if everybody messes up, everybody dies, passing forever from the face of the earth.

The word that springs to mind long about now is *instinct*, which the dictionary attempts to explain by using phrases such as "largely inheritable," "a complex response without involving reason," and "behavior below the conscious level." All that certainly sounds like the spider and the wasp, but it doesn't do much in the way of clarifying things. Reading between the lines in Webster's dictionary, we can see that Webster doesn't know what instinct is, either. So here it all rests for the time being until biologists can find out who or what is supplying the animals with their instructions.

> *"I can't explain myself, I'm afraid, sir,"*
> *said Alice, "because I'm not myself, you see."*
> *"I don't see," said the caterpillar.*

And neither do we.

CHAPTER 5

Blind Crossing

The wind blew hard across the Dakota territory, shaking the last of the summer flowers that fought valiantly to hold on. September clouds tumbled overhead and rushed to an unknown destination. The bison stirred.

It was getting late, and soon the biting snows would spill down from Canada, burying the land over which the great beasts roamed. Sometimes, although the native people never learned why, the animals would stay, their thick bodies hunched against the freezing winter. The snow would cling to their massive shoulders where it would turn to ice shafts and hang like heavy jeweled necklaces. Through the blinding gale, the Indians could just make out the young calves, small only in comparison to their parents, bending inward toward the great warming flanks as they sought protection from the fury. Somehow, the bison would last the winter.

But this year, like most, the bison felt the wind change direction and carry away the final days of summer. Slowly, the herds began to gather. Blindly driven by an ancestral urge, they came together until there were two hundred, five hundred, eight hundred thousand head filling the plain and stretching to the horizon. Their shaggy, muscular bodies rippled brown against the orange hills, and their cloven hooves crushed the sage and the scrub pine. A waning sun bowed its head, and the bison advanced in steady and thunderous determination across the land.

They moved southward toward Louisiana and Mexico and were joined by other herds from Kansas, Oklahoma, and Nebraska. The ranks swelled: a million, 2 million animals, black eyes staring straight ahead, flowing bodies wedged tightly like jigsaw-puzzle pieces.

From the forts along the bisons' route, the white man watched in awe at what the Sioux had seen so many times and turned to their advantage with bow and arrow. From a distance it looked like a smoky fire eating its way over the prairie. Powerful legs threw up a choking blanket of dust that billowed outward along the ground and all but engulfed the beasts.

As the migration grew nearer, the soldiers felt the air shake with the pounding of two million bison mindlessly pushing southward, undeterred by obstacles and drenching rains and unable to reverse direction because of the enormous size of the herd. On into Texas and New Mexico they drove for the rich grassland that had months ago vanished in the north. In the course of a single year, the bison would cross and recross many hundreds of miles in their instinctual quest for food. Their routes would always be the same, varying by just a few miles.

Today there are only a few thousand bison left. Men with names like Billy Comstock and Buffalo Bill and Broken Arrow lay in wait for the migrating herds and all but slaughtered them into extinction. Sadly, the handful of beasts that remain no longer make their annual trek southward. Perhaps there are not enough left to remember. . . .

If you have never actually seen a migration, you have at least heard stories—of the swallows that faithfully return each year to Capistrano or the annual salmon run when countless numbers of adult salmon relentlessly push their way upstream to spawn. Season after season, animals as diverse as caribou and bats, butterflies and seals, move with the advance of winter, the coming of sexual maturity, to another location. For some, it is a fantastic voyage fraught with obstacles and dangers. For others, it is little more than a leisurely stroll. For all, however, it is an ancient ritual, a pattern of survival deeply ingrained in the species and guided by the mysterious hand of nature.

We know very little about this journey called migration. Why do the countless generations of swallows always go to the little town of San Juan Capistrano and not Dana Point, which is right next to it? What landmarks, what clues, show the wheatear how to cross the Bering Strait, the Soviet Union, and a large portion of Africa to reach its final destination ten thousand miles from its starting point in North America? And perhaps most baffling of all, how do the mouse-eared bat, the albatross, the springbok, the lowly dragonfly, and all the others know when it is time to migrate? Is there a chemical trigger, a receptor of some sort, that works unfailingly to send the animals on their way?

Overhead we see a V formation of graceful Canada geese, calling, perhaps, in joyous liberation as they head north. The Canadas are migrating. We comment on their steady flight, their strength and precision. But we do not know why they always arrive as dependably as the setting sun. The animals are on the move, and if we are to gain at least some understanding of their annual passages, we must follow them.

Far beyond the colorful reefs where wide-eyed vacationers snorkel and the sunlight filters out to browns and darkness, the spiny lobsters assemble for their eerie midnight march. As the moon rises over the beaches many fathoms above, the lobsters crawl from their rocky dens and line up like schoolchildren going to lunch. Some lines are long and sinuous with fifty or sixty individuals delicately poised in antennae-to-tail contact. Other lines are curiously short, with just two or three lobsters. In a high-up place, the moon spills over the land. The lobsters move out, drenched in total blackness, guided by some unknown chart that will take them hundreds of miles from the Florida coast. Past Grand Bahama Island they will pour, toward Bimini, just skirting the 100-fathom line. Where are they going? No one knows, but the lobsters will not be diverted from their course. Scrabbling along the soft sand, they will brave autumn squalls and hurricanes, logging as much as fifty miles in a week. The lobstermen, of course, await these strange migrations with great anticipation, and their greed has severely depleted the population of the southern lobster. But enough females manage to get through, and the species survives.

The midnight migration of the spiny lobster is one of the most extraordinary journeys in the animal kingdom and today remains virtually unexplained. Marine biologists have no real idea where the spiny lobster eventually winds up or how long the march lasts. They can only guess that because the lobster is a nocturnal animal, its migration is governed to a large part by the waxing and waning hours of daylight, even though the lobsters certainly cannot see the change from their 100-fathom depth.

Biologists also guess that one purpose of the migration is redistribution. As the population rises, food naturally becomes harder and harder to find, although lobsters are remarkably adaptable. They enjoy clams, hermit crabs, sea urchins, and starfish, but if any or all of the above is unavailable, the lobster will easily switch over to sea cucumbers.*

The lobsters also may migrate to new breeding grounds that will perhaps be free of their main preditors—jewfish, triggerfish, octopuses, and sharks. Nearly all of the lobsters studied during migratory marches were either sexually mature or nearly so. The conclusion, then, would seem to be that the lobsters shift territory in preparation for egg laying.

In addition to tackling the inky darkness, the spiny lobster quite often begins its strange march smack in the wake of furious weather. When Hurricane Betsy struck the Bahamas in 1965, spiny lobsters "swarmed across the Bahama Banks like a locust plague," according to one fisherman. Do lobsters "read" the storms as indications of the arrival of autumn?

Maybe the greatest mystery of all, however, is how the spiny lobsters find their way through what is the equivalent of a howling sandstorm in the middle of a moonless night. The effects of a really bad hurricane can be felt many, many feet below the surface of the ocean. Indeed, if the storm is severe enough, it will churn up the sand on the bottom until the waters several fathoms down become even wilder than the weather on the surface. But despite the fact that the lobsters are pounded and buf-

---

*Despite its name, the sea cucumber is not a vegetable but a cucumber-shaped animal that feels a lot like a water balloon. Many species are toxic, but the spiny lobster fortunately can tell which is which.

feted, pushed and pummeled, they somehow always manage to get where they are going. Surely they must use some sort of clues or landmarks. Or perhaps they have a way of taking directional readings, because they never lose their way and, more amazingly, push onward hour after hour with fierce determination.

Scientists have found a structure in fish called a lateral line, which tells the animal when there is a pressure change in its immediate neighborhood. This is why a goldfish does not bump into the sides of its tank. Lobsters, however, are not fish. They are crustaceans, which means that instead of having an internal skeleton, they are completely enclosed in a shell-like covering called an exoskeleton.* So far as the marine biologists can tell, lobsters do not have a lateral line or any other kind of structure that could serve as a migration compass. So how do the spiny lobsters manage to cross such vast distances under some of the worst possible traveling conditions?

If the spiny lobster's deep-sea march is amazing, consider the extraordinary migration of the freshwater eel. Freshwater eels, also called yellow eels, are found throughout Europe in everything from rivers to ponds. About the only thing that is not mysterious about their migration is its purpose. The eels become sexually mature when they are about six years old. This change

---

*Clams and oysters are also enclosed in shells, but they are not crustaceans. They are bivalves, meaning that the animal is found tucked inside two shells attached by a muscular hinge.

inside them is marked by a very sudden change in color. Decked out now in a shiny silver, the eels immediately begin their long journey to the ocean where they will eventually mate. For some, however, just getting started is a remarkable feat.

Eels that live in rivers that empty into the Atlantic simply follow the river to its outflow. But many eels are landlocked. They live in lakes and ponds that are virtually in the middle of nowhere, far from rivers that would give them direct access to the ocean. So the eels wait for a rainy night to make their departure. When the ground is sodden, they emerge from the water and travel by land—sometimes for many miles—until they come either to a river or the Atlantic coast.

The eels' overland journey becomes even more impressive when you stop to consider the fact that eels are not snakes, but true fish, complete with gills. While a snake feels perfectly comfortable rustling through meadow grasses or sidewinding across the desert, an eel decidedly does not. Eels breathe by extracting oxygen from the water, so this is why they will not begin their migration as long as the land is dry. But the story gets even better.

The eels, which may come from as far away as Scandanavia and the Mediterranean, are headed for the Sargasso Sea, the setting for countless myths and legends. The Sargasso lies in the North Atlantic between the West Indies and the Azores, a handful of Portuguese islands that once served as a place of exile for criminals.

The Sargasso also sits right in the middle of the horse latitudes.

The horse latitudes got their name during the days when ships had to rely exclusively on wind to get anywhere (unless there was a contingent of slaves who could do the rowing). Often, horses were transported as cargo, and when the winds died, as they almost always did around the Azores, the horses had to be thrown overboard to save the meager supplies of water. A ship could be becalmed for days on end, so sailors understandably dreaded a voyage that would take them through the horse latitudes.

The Sargasso Sea is an eerie site of calm in a part of the Atlantic where a number of crosscurrents converge. The currents are unusually strong and form a kind of vortex. Like the serene eye of a hurricane, the Sargasso Sea barely moves, and on its surface floats a jungle of gulfweed, or sargasso weed, a greenish brown seaweed that can grow quite long.

Seaweed is slimy stuff and will easily entwine a swimmer, but the gulfweed in the Sargasso Sea is particularly nasty because there is so much of it. This combination of a mad vortex topped by deceptively still water choked with strange plants has given rise to the legend of the Bermuda triangle. Bermuda trianglers claim that for years, everything from fighter planes to ocean liners have been vanishing without a trace in the haunted waters of the Sargasso Sea. Only the eels don't seem to be bothered by the area's bad reputation because each summer they head straight for the same spawning grounds they always have used.

They arrive in uncountable numbers, having traveled ten miles a day nonstop for nine months. And if that isn't difficult enough, the entire journey is made without guideposts or landmarks of any kind. Somehow the eels are able to cross a sizable chunk of the Atlantic Ocean at a depth of 1,000 fathoms (6,000 feet)—a truly staggering accomplishment.

It is unlikely that the eels use celestial clues to help them on their way, primarily because no animal can see the stars and moon from six thousand feet below the surface of the water. So scientists have speculated that the eel's lateral-line symmetry plays a role in orienting the animals. In fresh water, eels have shown a sensitivity to electrical fields as weak as one millivolt per centimeter.* In salt water, however, the eels can detect fields of a quadrillionth of a volt!

Now, the earth, as you probably already know, is surrounded by a vast magnetic field, and water is an excellent conductor of electricity. As the water flows past the earth's magnetic lines of force, it sets up a current that the eels are able to detect via their lateral-line organs. The eels can then orient themselves with respect to the ocean currents. But that's only half the story.

When the larvae are born into the pitch darkness, they

---

*A standard wall outlet in the United States delivers 110 volts of electricity. This is able to run your hair dryer and power the TV. One millivolt is 1/1,000th of a volt.

are barely a quarter of an inch long and no thicker than a pencil line, yet they immediately head for the surface. Once on top, they begin their long, long journey toward the European continent. It will take them three years, and in all that time they will have grown just three inches. Still immature, they somehow find their way to the freshwater rivers and streams from which their parents came (although not necessarily the same ones), and there they will remain until their biological clock directs them to return again to the sea.

Why the eels go to all this trouble is a mystery. If the eels must spawn in salt water, why not pick something a little closer—say, the North Sea, or the Mediterranean, or the Bay of Biscay? What can possibly be the benefit of traveling all those miles?

Actually, many migrating animals almost seem to flaunt their ability to cover extraordinary distances. French biologist Matthieu Ricard reports that common European coots have logged hundreds of miles in an extremely short period of time. One bird, says Ricard, crossed 450 miles in just thirty-six hours.

The swift is a small and somewhat unspectacular bird, but its migratory feats are not. Once it sets out, it does not touch land until the end of its journey many thousands of miles away. As darkness falls upon the European landscape, the swifts begin their ascent, spiraling in ever-widening circles, higher and higher, and then circling the area as if to establish their bearings. Then all at once, they seem able to see the route in their mind's eye, and they immediately pour southward, never varying from their course and never stopping.

The swift flies at the dizzying height of six thousand feet, more than a mile up, and in this way avoids many dangers and obstacles. Within a single season, it travels the entire length of the African continent to its winter home on the Cape of Good Hope, over both desert and ocean, resting only when it is able to ride a favorable air current.

The golden plover is a shorebird that makes what is called a loop migration; it travels in a southeast route at the end of the summer and returns in the fall via a wide, arcing northwesterly path. In summer golden plovers are found along the coast of Labrador in eastern Canada, but they winter in Brazil, making their yearly round-trip in excess of twelve thousand miles!

However, it is the Arctic tern that holds the distance record. As its name implies, the Arctic tern nests in the northernmost parts of Europe, North America, and Siberia, close to the North Pole. This slender-beaked seabird was once thought to be flightless as a juvenile and only to earn its wings, so to speak, as it matured. So it came as quite a revelation when one of the young birds that had been banded on the coast of Labrador in northern Canada turned up three months later in southern Africa.

The Arctic tern's amazing migration takes it literally from one pole to the other. At the end of the summer it leaves its colonies in the far north and travels either a

Pacific route or follows the coastlines of western Europe and Africa until it reaches the shorelines of Antarctica. The one-way trip is over ten thousand miles, covering an entire hemisphere. With the coming of spring, the birds return to the Arctic, making their annual migration a staggering twenty thousand miles long!

The migration of the monarch butterfly, one of the most beautiful sights in nature, is no less impressive. This seemingly fragile insect, noted for its startling orange-red wings veined in violet and flecked with white, measures just four inches across. Yet, in the 1850s, American monarchs were able to reach the island of Hawaii, two thousand miles away. They have further spread to Borneo and New Zealand, all under their own flight power.

Another insect, the locust, migrates both by air and land, depending on its stage of growth. Just after the spring rains, the locust hatches from a tiny egg as a wingless grasshopper. Normally, the grasshopper is a solitary creature, content to feed on the available vegetation and mind its own business. But if the climate is good and nourishing rains enrich the land, the grasshopper population begins to swell to ungainly proportions. Each spring brings more and more grasshoppers that are soon competing for food. Once bountiful, the land can now no longer support the steadily increasing numbers of grasshoppers. One day, the community reaches its breaking point, and without warning, the grasshoppers begin to migrate.

At first, the hoppers are barely noticeable, advancing across the land in small groups. But before long, the groups are joined by other, larger groups, and as the teeming insects merge, they begin to cover the ground like a flood, sweeping over everything in their path. They are unstoppable now, driven to press onward through towns and cities and over rivers that they cross by forming a living suspension bridge. The advance guard literally flings itself into the water where the individual hoppers arrange themselves one behind the other until they have stretched from shore to shore. Bouncing and weaving like a flimsy rope bridge high in the Andes, the grasshoppers support the marching hoards, which may number well into the many millions.

The solitary grasshopper can cover a hundred miles or more in its migration and it relentlessly pushes forward in search of food. But it is the locust that strikes fear into the hearts of farmers and townspeople alike. When the locust swarms, it is an unforgettable sight.

Locusts are essentially winged grasshoppers, and their ability to fly makes their migration both spectacular and horrible. In the Book of Exodus, a swarm of locusts was said to have "covered the face of the whole earth" so that "there remained not any green thing, either tree or herb of the field, through all the land of Egypt." This description is probably not exaggeration. A migrating swarm can have as many as 10 billion individuals that sweep over the fields and attack the vegetation in a frenzy of feeding. In a frighteningly short time, branches and stalks are stripped clean, the grass completely devoured, farms laid to waste, and then, like some evil alien life form, the locusts rise up and move off. Their teeming numbers are astounding, dense enough to form a thick cloud that blocks out the sun and casts a shadow over the land. Locust clouds have been measured as wide as twelve miles!

In direct contrast to most migrations, which seem the very spirit of freedom and harmony with nature, is the strange and disturbing march of the lemmings. This infamous trek is neither an annual migration nor does it take the animal to a more desirable feeding ground. It is, instead, an exodus, a mass evacuation in which all roads lead to death. For many years, biologists were at a complete loss to explain the lemmings' behavior. It seemed to go against everything they knew about the animal will to survive. Because the lemmings were traveling in huge numbers over large tracts of land on a somewhat regular basis, their march was, by definition, a migration. But it certainly bore no resemblance to the migrations of other animals whose journeys clearly benefited the group. What, thought the scientists, were they to make of the lemmings?

The lemming is a small rodent found mostly in Scandinavia. It has a light beige coat with a wide, black shoulder marking and a very thin stripe down the back. Lemmings are rather appealing-looking little creatures. Round and fluffy, tailess, with delicate white whiskers and dark eyes, they keep pretty much to themselves. They feed on whatever is available at the time, from seeds to insects, and are well adapted to the long, cold winters of Norway and Finland.

Lemmings normally give birth to four or five young each year. Since births and deaths for the most part cancel each other out, the population remains stable and the land can provide sufficient food for everyone. But every so often, something apparently goes wrong, and the number of births suddenly explodes. Seven, eight, even nine offspring are produced as many as five times in a season, far more than the available resources can support. Somehow, the lemmings sense the imbalance, but they do not migrate to richer ground. Instead, they begin to move toward the sea.

They come in a trickle at first, and then by the hundreds, from the hills and highlands, flowing together to form larger and larger groups that sweep over the plains like waves. Shy and timid the year before, they are now violent and aggressive and driven with single-minded purpose. Undeterred by obstacles, they sweep over everything in their path, brazenly pouring into towns and entering houses through doorways, windows, chinks in the walls, spilling into rivers that they cross in a blind frenzy. They push onward robotlike, scrambling up and over the sides of boats, across the decks, and down into the water again. During their terrible death march, the lemmings will cover an astonishing fifteen miles a day, every day, until they at last reach the sea.

The dark, icy waters lap against the beach, drawing the lemmings in. One after the other, the lemmings plunge into the churning waves and continue their journey, swimming for a place that perhaps lies old and faded in their dim collective memories. But the sea is too vast, and hundreds of thousands of lemmings will die before any could possibly reach the opposite shore.

Where, the scientists wonder, would the lemmings eventually wind up if they were not stopped by the sea? Some believe the lemmings are following an ancient migration route that took their ancestors to the British Isles. Before water filled in the land and became the North Sea, the lemmings easily could have crossed back and forth between Britain and Norway. In fact, some of the animals have actually reached the Lofoten Islands whose distance to the mainland of Norway ranges from one to fifty miles. Instead of committing mass suicide, couldn't the lemmings be responding exactly as their ancestors did, seeking a more fertile feeding ground for their explosive population?

Scientists have charted the principal lemming migration routes on a map of Scandinavia, and every track shows the lemmings heading directly for a major body of water. From northern Finland and Sweden, the lemmings move either toward the Atlantic Ocean or the Gulf of Bothnia in the Baltic Sea. Lemmings that start out farther south, near Oslo, Norway, travel overland until they reach the North Sea. From Finmark in Norway they go to the Arctic Ocean. These patterns hardly suggest an attempt to reach the British Isles. In fact, while the routes vary, the destinations do not; they are always the sea. So the lemming march seems deliberate. But why?

Studies with rats have shown very remarkable behavior changes when the population reaches suffocating proportions. Food supplies, once perfectly adequate, now cannot support even a small fraction of the community. Too many rats in too small a space leads to a breakdown in the social structure. The females lose interest in the young and fail to care for them properly. The infant mortality rate rises sharply and can reach 95 percent. The rats become fierce and aggressive, and wars break out, resulting in many casualties.

Scientists have suggested that a sudden population explosion triggers this same behavior in the lemmings. Powerless to reestablish the social order, the lemmings have no choice but to wipe the slate clean with a mass suicide. Of course, not all the lemmings die, but a tremendous number succumb to the waves.

Nature seems terribly cruel in this instance, but in the long run the species survives—which is what counts. So despite what the lemmings' death march looks like, it is really no different than any other migration. Those left behind have more food, and generations that follow are stronger and healthier.

As the eerie march of the lemmings illustrates, there are many secrets left to be discovered about migration. Truly baffling, for example, is what seems to be some sort of ESP in the springbok, a beautiful African gazelle whose numbers have sadly diminished through the years. Once the springbok were plentiful, grazing the high ground of southern Africa and moving great distances in their annual migrations. The springbok followed the seasons. They wintered in the hills of the southwest where frequent rains brought nourishment to the land and provided young shoots for the newborn calves. But as the season wore on and the rains came less often, the springbok moved to the north and east. There spring rains had filled the pools and stimulated new growth, and food was again plentiful.

The springbok's annual migrations may well have been triggered by the dwindling food supply combined with a change in the climate. As their immediate environment altered—even subtly—the springbok took note and shifted location. But there must have been other clues for them, too, because whenever the rains failed in the north, the springbok remained in the south. Somehow they sensed the dry conditions hundreds of miles away and knew that a migration that year would be of no benefit, so they stayed put. When the rains returned the following year, they migrated. What kind of internal "radar" can detect the weather on the other side of a continent?

Animals, of course, do not know that spring begins on March 1 in the Northern Hemisphere. They couldn't care less that Labor Day marks the end of summer for many of us. But they are aware that the days are changing, even when the heat of August lasts well into September and sometimes October. Animals use the oldest calendar in the world—the sun—to tell them when it is time to begin their migrations.

Because our planet follows a slightly elliptical path around the sun and because the earth is tilted on its axis, days and nights are of varying length throughout the year. Experiments have shown that animals are remarkably sensitive to this gradual shortening and lengthening of the day. Indeed, ground squirrels and other hibernators rely on these light clues to tell them when it is time to tuck in for the winter. Migrating birds respond to the changes first by increasing their fat deposits in preparation for their long flight. The signal to leave may actually be internal (chemical), but there is little doubt that the light of the sun is a migratory trigger. In fact, several species consistently leave well in advance of the cold weather. This is not being wimpy, but rather it's a long-conditioned response to the waning daylight hours.

If animals don't need calendars and almanacs, they don't need road maps, compasses, or sextants, either. Most reach their destination, even if it is many hundreds of miles from their starting point. Furthermore, they get there under overcast skies, in the middle of the night, through blinding snowstorms, over acres of trackless desert, and in pitch blackness a thousand fathoms down.

When scientists first observed bees doing their so-called "waggle dance," they guessed (correctly) that the bees were giving directions to a newly discovered food source. But even better was the fact that the dancing bee was using the sun's position in the sky to create a kind of geometry. "Draw a straight line from the hive to the sun," said the bee in its dance, "and then measure a hundred twenty-degree angle." Or perhaps, "Draw a line through the midpoint of my dance to the hive. Measure thirty degrees to form a right angle and there you will find the food source." If this is all quite incredible, still more amazing is the bee's ability to adjust its dance as the sun moves across the sky. The bee gets assistance from its internal clock, which records the waning of the day with remarkable precision.

So it should come as no surprise that migrating animals use not only the sun as a guide, but the moon, the stars, the earth's magnetic field, sonar and echolocation—bouncing sound waves off objects—and even their own sense of smell! When the golden plover takes off for the Hawaiian Islands, its fix on the target must be absolutely perfect. If it miscalculates by just one degree, it will be off about one mile for every sixty miles of flight. Since the golden plover starts out in Alaska, a one-degree mistake could put it smack in the middle of the Pacific Ocean.

When an albatross was released from an island off the coast of Washington State, it somehow found its way back to its nesting site on Midway Island in the Pacific. Just glance at a map and you will immediately see that the bird had to fly exclusively over water. What did it use for landmarks?

Nocturnal migrants—birds, especially—appear to be using the stars, just as the ancient sailors did. Warblers, brightly colored little birds known for their songs (hence the name), won't take off until they have lined themselves up in the direction of their flight. Then they go. If there is a heavy cloud cover, the warblers stay put until there is a break. They need only about ten or fifteen stars to orient themselves, the equivalent of two constellations for the early sailors.

How the warblers and others actually use the stars is yet to be resolved, though. Certainly they don't calculate altitude and azimuth and latitude and longitude and sidereal time and celestial time and local time and Greenwich time and then submit a flight plan. But they most definitely know just where they are.

Intrigued by migrating birds' celestial navigational skills, Dr. Franz Sauer brought a group of whitethroats into the Olbers Planetarium in Bremen, West Germany. With a flip of a switch, Sauer reproduced the night sky on the ceiling, exactly as it was right overhead outside the planetarium on that very evening. Sauer released the birds, which immediately responded by turning to face the southeast, just as they would have if they had been outside and preparing for flight.

But this, Sauer thought, was no big deal. "Let's see how good astronomers they really are!" Almost devilishly, Sauer rotated the star dome 180 degrees. He literally turned the world upside down on the birds, putting them into the Southern Hemisphere. Gone were the familiar stars of the Big and Little dippers, of Draco and Cassiopeia. Instead, the birds were looking at the Southern Cross and constellations with strange names like Pavo, the Peacock. Ancient sailors who spent their entire careers in northern waters would have jumped ship, but the whitethroats were as cool as could be. They simply turned around until they were facing northwest, the precise opposite of the way they would have faced, had Sauer not messed up the sky.

Round and round went the planetarium ceiling as Sauer tried again and again to trick the birds. But the whitethroats were not to be denied, and in every instance, they made the correct compensation. At last, Sauer did the only thing left to be done; he switched off the lights. The planetarium sky fell dark as though a great cloud had descended upon the land. Not a wing rustled. Not a feather stirred. The whitethroats were waiting for the skies to clear.

Snow geese seem to rely on a variety of navigational aids. They will fly regardless of the time of day or the weather. Above or below the clouds, or even submerged *in* the clouds, the snow geese make their way northward to their spring breeding grounds along the Arctic coast. Scientists are quite certain that the geese are using the sun and stars as well as large ground landmarks when the skies are clear, and their own built-in magnetic field sensors when clouds obscure their view.

The idea that animals might be sensitive to the magnetic field of the earth at first struck most scientists as fantastic, but recent experiments have turned up some rather fascinating information. Termite queens, for instance, consistently align themselves in either an east/west position—perpendicular to the earth's magnetic poles—or north/south—parallel to the poles, although why they do this remains a mystery.

In 1957, Dr. Hans Fromme, working at the Frankfort Zoological Institute, learned that European robins not only can detect the earth's magnetic field, but also use it to determine flight direction during their annual migration. As things stand now, however, nobody has the slightest idea how the robins, snow geese, and others actually use this data to create flight plans for themselves.

On the face of it, navigation by bouncing sound waves off an object (echolocation) seems pretty clear and straightforward. Most bats, as you know, do this sort of thing all the time. Unconcerned by blackness, the bats emit a series of high-pitched squeaks that return to them after having been deflected by objects in their vicinity. The bats then get a highly detailed sonar map that serves them just as well as eyesight. (Contrary to popular belief, though, bats are not blind.)

Anyone who has spent a summer at sleep-away camp has probably seen these nocturnal pilots swooping and gliding through the eaves of the bunk. Their sharp flapping, like the snap of a wet sheet on a clothesline, along with tales of bats entangling themselves in people's hair, has sent scores of campers running for cover. But as long as a bat can squeak it will never crash, let alone dive into someone's pigtails. Its radar is so remarkable, the bat can maneuver around rocky overhangs while catching tiny insects in midflap. Bats are truly sensational aviators, with the ability to echolocate objects almost as thin as a human hair—7/100ths of a millimeter.

Just avoiding rock overhangs and other bats, however, is hardly the same thing as navigating five hundred miles from southeastern Europe to central Russia or over seven hundred miles of dry scrub and sagebrush into southern Mexico. You certainly have to wonder just how the bats are interpreting their radar map. Are they encoded with instructions that tell them to "turn five degrees south-southeast three seconds after you pass the third valley"? Recognizing that something is a mountain and knowing that you're supposed to cross it are two entirely different things.

Even more mysterious is how whales use echolocation on their annual migrations. A humpback whale may cover four thousand miles in a season, traveling from the warm tropical waters where it breeds to the frigid seas of the Antarctic. If echolocation shows whales the way, off what do they bounce their sounds? There aren't too many distinguishing characteristics in the middle of the ocean. In fact, once past Cape Town in South Africa, land masses thin out to just a few scattered islands. Since whales are mammals and must breathe air, they often breach, that is, leap out of the water. If they use this opportunity to take a sighting, what do they sight?

But maybe the greatest puzzle is how baby cuckoos find their way from Europe to Africa all by themselves. In what is certainly one of nature's more unusual ideas, the adult cuckoos lay their eggs in other birds' nests. Then they are off to do whatever it is grown-up cuckoos do before heading south for the winter. Meanwhile, most of the foster parents think nothing of these instant adoption proceedings and sit on the cuckoo eggs right along with their own. The cuckoo mothers never look back and never learn what it is that eventually hatches from their eggs. By July, the baby cuckoos are feeding from their foster mothers at a furious pace while their birth mothers are halfway to Africa.

Odd as all of this seems, the foster mothers accept the responsibility of cuckoo child rearing, and the baby cuckoos thrive. They are even taught to fly by their rent-a-moms, and so when August finally unfolds, the young cuckoos are ready for their first major flight. This, however, just happens to be a migratory flight for which they have absolutely no preparation. Not a single cuckoo among them has any prior experience, and all the grown-ups who know the route have been gone for weeks. The foster families certainly can't supply any information about the wintering grounds of the common cuckoo, so they are of no help. And yet, somehow the baby cuckoos reach Africa, unfailingly, year after year after year. So we have to ask ourselves: What is the trick?

Up to now we have been looking for external clues

that show migratory animals the route they're supposed to take. But suppose all the details are on biology's version of the computer chip? Suppose the map is genetically encoded, as body structure, fur and feather markings, tail length, and all the rest are preprogrammed into the genes? The stars and geographical characteristics, then, would only serve as signposts along the way; the animal innately knows just where it is going—with or without an instructor.

Migration, as common as it is in the animal kingdom, is far from understood. And the ebb and flow of the animals, like the tides, raises some provocative questions about our roots. How, indeed, did we get here, and where are we going? Perhaps ours, too, is just a blind crossing.

CHAPTER 6

All Fall Down

A ll fall down," for those of you who have forgotten, is the last line of "Ring around the Rosie," a grim little rhyme if ever there was one. "Ring around the Rosie" was actually born during the plague years in London, 1664 to 1665. Children would chant the words as they watched the death carts, piled high with grotesquely swollen bodies, slowly make their way down rat-infested streets.

The original line was "Ring-o-ring o' roses," referring to the circular red skin rash that signaled the onset of the disease. It was the kiss of death. Terrified, the people took to carrying around herbs—the "pocket full of posies"—in hopes of warding off the infection. The third line of the rhyme, "Ashes, ashes," originated as the sneeze words "A-tishoo! A-tishoo!" and the last line, of course, was a statement about the death toll—"All fall down."

While this chapter is not about the Black Death, it does have something to do with plagues, or at least things that used to pass for plagues.

Somewhere in the vicinity of 2500 B.C., Moses, so the biblical story goes, was trying to negotiate a treaty with the pharoah of Egypt. The Israelites were being held in bondage, and Moses wanted an unconditional release. When the pharaoh told Moses for about the tenth time just to forget the whole thing, Moses appealed to God to do something scary. Immediately, God came up with the idea of plagues.

Being a gentleman, Moses gave the pharaoh ample warning, but the pharaoh was conceited and just snorted. "Hit me with your best shot," he said, or words to that effect. So Moses shrugged, gave God the all clear sign, and in the flash of an instant it started to rain frogs.

This certainly would have convinced most people to release the Israelites, but the pharaoh was something of a tough customer. He might even have said, "Go ahead, make my day," which God did by sending a storm of locusts.

Now, the story of Exodus is quite a fantastic tale, made even more colorful by all the strange stuff that fell out of the sky on top of the pharaoh's head. But the story of Exodus is also probably not fantasy, and its credibility comes from perhaps the most unlikely part—the plagues. Frogs, locusts, and a whole variety of exotic creatures have been raining on people's heads for years; for over twenty-five hundred years, in fact—since the time of the Exodus.

It was on a Saturday in June 1954 when Sylvia Mowday took her two young children to see an exhibition by the Royal Navy in a nearby park. After the exhibition, the children urged Mrs. Mowday to take them to the fair that had been set up on the other side of the park. They began to cross the green when all of a sudden, a terrific rain storm broke out.

"We tried to reach a belt of trees," said Mrs. Mowday, "and my four-year-old put her little red umbrella up and we heard these things thudding against it."

To the Mowday family's astonishment, it was not rain or hail that beat so furiously against the little red umbrella, but hundreds of thousands of tiny frogs. In no time at all, the umbrella was covered, as were the Mowdays' shoes and the ground around the Mowdays' feet.

But this is nothing. In August 1944, the Pittman family was out for a walk in the English Midlands. All at once the sky darkened and it began to pour—first rain, then frogs.

Nineteen sixty-nine. Buckinghamshire, England. *London Sunday Express* reporter Veronica Papworth witnesses a rain of frogs as she is dressing for a dinner party. Having left the windows of her home wide open, Papworth is somewhat unnerved to find that the frogs are raining into her living room.

England by no means has an exclusive on frog rains. Over the years, investigator of the strange Charles Fort collected dozens and dozens of reports from all over the world. There is the baffling frog fall in a dry-as-dust desert region in Nevada as well as an account that goes all the way back to ancient Greece. The very esteemed journal *Nature* reported a 1915 frog fall on the island of Gibraltar, and in Decmeber 1977, the *London Sunday Times* carried the story of a frog fall in the Sahara Desert!

There is more to all of this than you might think, however. In addition to frogs, large and small, the sky also seems to dump an interesting variety of fish on people's heads. A thirteen-inch herring fell out of a perfectly clear sky in Buffalo, New York, and a shower of fish, including a squid, rained down on the city of Boston. Kershaw County in South Carolina was pelted with catfish and perch in 1901, and what was described as a "heavy shower" of herring drenched the Odd Fellows Cemetery in Sacramento in 1879. Freakish events? Hardly.

E. W. Gudger of the American Museum of Natural History in New York City began collecting reports of fish falls just after the turn of the century. By 1946, he had seventy-eight stories, which averages to about two a year. But those are just fish falls.

Consider the water lizards that fell on Utah, the alligator that landed at the corner of Wentworth and Anson streets in Charleston, South Carolina, and the crabs, eels, snakes, worms, caterpillars, turtles, snails, and even birds that have tumbled out of the sky either singly or en masse. It's enough to make you want to reinforce your umbrella with steel beams.

Scientist William Corliss is the modern-day Charles Fort. (Fort died in 1932.) For quite some time now, Corliss has been investigating the bizarre and the unexplained in nature, and he states without hesitation that animal sky falls are not hokum; they do, indeed, occur. Witnesses range from tipsy patrons of English pubs (unreliable) to meteorologists and other scientists (very reliable). There is nothing secret and shadowy about the falls, either. They do not happen under the cover of darkness or along deserted stretches of road. In 1877, *Scientific American* reported a fall of live snakes, twelve to eighteen inches long, in Memphis, Tennessee. A local weather report corroborated the story: "Morning opened with light rain. Ten-twenty A.M. Began to pour down in torrents, lasting fifteen minutes, wind southwest. Immediately after, the reptiles were discovered crawling on the sidewalks, in the road, gutters, and yards of Vance Street between Landerdale and Goslee streets."

As with any strange phenomenon, however, not all witnesses can be said to be 100 percent reliable. You always will have a handful of pub patrons with an extra pint of ale in them—and just plain liars. But animal rains occur right out in the open where there are usually loads of passersby. And because they are classified as meteorological events, they have the attention of scientists and weather forecasters. So while some reports may be a bit exaggerated, the vast majority can be taken at face value; they are what they have been reported to be.

But what exactly are they?

Many experts usually answer that question by saying that animal rains are caused by whirlwinds and waterspouts that appear out of nowhere, suck up their hapless victims, carry them miles away, and drop them on unsuspecting cities and towns. This would explain why it often rains just before a frog or fish or salamander or squid falls. It does not, however, explain about half a dozen other characteristics of the falls.

First, whirlwinds and waterspouts are not selective in their catch. They scoop up whatever is in the water—not only fish of all kinds and sizes, but rocks, sand, seaweed, and other debris. Whirlwinds and waterspouts are low-pressure, extremely violent storms that rotate very rapidly like tornadoes. They form over open water and thus pull into their funnels huge amounts of sea life and anything else that isn't nailed down (and sometimes things that are).

Yet most animal rains deposit only one species, either all frogs, all mackerel, and so on. Rarely does it look like a fish market after an animal rain. In addition, algae, seaweed, barnacles, sand, and other gifts from the sea are conspicuously absent. How can a waterspout send the fish but hold back the rocks and vegetables?

Then there is the problem of the rain itself. If a waterspout is at work, the rain that falls should be the water that formed the spout. We can tell what kind of water formed the spout based on the fish. If they are saltwater fish, we conclude the spout formed over a body of salt water, probably the ocean. But whenever someone has had the presence of mind to test the water from an animal rain, it's always been found to be fresh water *even when the fish deposited have been saltwater fish!*

Something else the waterspout theory cannot account for is the occasional fall of land animals. This is not to suggest that elephants and rhinos are coming down, but there have been reports of caterpillars, worms, and as mentioned above, snakes. Now, common sense tells you that waterspouts are not transporting these animals. So what is? Dust devils, maybe? Tornadoes?

The next story, though, will prove beyond a shadow of a doubt why the waterspout theory needs some serious work. The scene of the fall was Marksville, Louisiana, a small, cozy town with a population of about four thousand. On the morning of October 23, 1947, the good citizens of Marksville awoke to a downpour of largemouth bass that filled the streets at an alarming rate. Present, too, were minnows, two species of sunfish, and hickory shad, all freshwater fish native to local waters.

Now, so far this sounds like the work of a waterspout, but something was conspicuously absent. It never rained in Marksville that day. The weather was gray and foggy, but the fog could hardly be called pea soup. Winds were light, about six to eight miles an hour, and the weather service had no reports of tornadoes or unusual storm activity in the region, although the day before several dust devils had been sighted. Dust devils are a land phenomenon, and so for them to have played a part, we have to imagine the little devils jumping into the water, sucking up the fish, and then hanging on to them for twenty-four hours.

The fish that fell on Marksville that day in October were fresh, and while one of the biologists from the Department of Wildlife and Fisheries went about preserving specimens in alcohol, everyone else scooped up armfuls and headed for their kitchens. A fresh fish fall in India resulted in a lot of curry dinners that night, and there is no telling how many falls went unrecorded because the townspeople ate the evidence.

Sometimes the fish come down frozen, which is very strange, unless it's because the whirlwind or tornado lifts them high enough to be frozen by the extremely low temperatures in the upper atmosphere.

There are also plenty of live falls, frogs creating the biggest sensation because they start hopping around almost as soon as they hit the ground. Chances are the live snake fall in Memphis, Tennessee, was also a bit unnerving. Whatever is transporting live cargo must be doing it very efficiently, not to mention gently.

In 1918, residents of Hendon, England, had to suffer through a dead-fish fall, but what is worth noting here is the length of time the fish had been dead. It was reported that the fish were "quite stiff," suggesting a condition of rigor mortis. Rigor mortis has a definite time schedule. It may begin as early as ten minutes after death or it may be delayed several hours.* Usually, however, the rigor mortis begins to wear off in about twenty-four hours, and it would not be present at all after thirty-six. So we can fix the time of death of the Hendon fish at no more than about thirty to thirty-six hours *before* they fell.

There is one more very curious characteristic of most of these fish and critter falls. Contrary to what you might expect, the animals fall in a very well-defined area, covering what can be described as a wide swath or long rectangular patch. The fish that fell in Marksville, Louisiana, covered an area that measured a thousand feet by eighty feet. In 1859, fish were reported to have fallen within the confines of an eighty- by twelve-yard strip. If there is anything significant about this pattern, scientists have yet to discover what it is.

The last word on animal rains certainly has to belong to the British astronomer Sir Fred Hoyle. In the 1970s, Hoyle, with the support of his colleague, Professor Chandra Wickramasinghe, shook up the scientific community when they proposed that life did not originate on the earth. Instead, said Hoyle and Wickramasinghe, our planet was "seeded" with living organisms from space. These microscopic creatures were carried into the sun's vicinity on comets. As the comets entered the inner solar

---

*The condition of the body, the cause of death, and atmospheric and climatic conditions all affect the onset of rigor mortis.

system, the sun's warmth began to boil off some of the ice and frozen gases, thereby liberating the freeze-dried organisms. The microaliens fell like rain upon the earth, went forth, multiplied, and became us.

A few years before, two astronomers announced that they had identified "microscopic-sized particles, resembling fossil algae, in relatively large quantities" in a meteorite that had fallen in France. It is known today as the Orgueil meteorite after its crash site, and it seems to suggest that a lot more exotic things than frogs and snakes can fall from the sky.

So maybe once upon a time, long, long ago, the animal rains were us. . . .

CHAPTER 7

I Shall Return!

It was a hot night in Cairo when the mad scientist slipped furtively into the tomb. The dust of centuries rose in yellow waves around him and settled in a fine layer on his rumpled lab coat. The scientist's eyes were fiery with creative passion, lighting up the inky crypt like the headlights on a '39 Dodge. Remembering the importance of sound effects, the scientist laughed diabolically as he pried open the gold lid of the pharaoh's sarcophagus. Naturally, it creaked.

The scientist gazed lovingly at the moldy mummy, which fortunately had had a hole left for the mouth. A few rapid heartbeats and then the scientist withdrew the nine sacred tanna leaves from the pocket of his coat. With great ceremony he dropped them into a goblet that just happened to be handy and held the goblet up to the mummy's gauzy lips.

"Drink deeply," said the mad scientist.

The mummy drank deeply.

Silence embraced the ancient crypt as the filmmakers allowed the tension to build. And then, when they figured the audience would be as close to the edge of their seats as they could come without sliding onto the floor, the mummy awoke.

"Cut! Print!" yelled the director, and the rest is motion-picture history. The film was a huge success and spawned a legion of sequels, which audiences paid the outrageous price of ten cents to see. Eyes wide and fingers greasy from the homemade chicken they had brought to the theater, the people sat absolutely transfixed by a foot-dragging mummy returned to life after twenty-five hundred years.

Nobody, of course, believed any of it. Certainly the producers knew it was fiction. The actors didn't buy it. Even the ancient Egyptians would have been skeptical, and it had all been their idea in the first place. But if you subtract the nine tanna leaves and take out a couple of other embellishments, you come to a rather eerie case of art imitating life.

Consider, for instance, the following story, retold from an 1879 report in *Scientific American:*

Professor Allen peered into the inky depths of the well. "How long has it been closed?" he asked, squinting into the darkness.

"Twenty years," came the reply. "Ever since the water dried up. Now there's nothing down there but a thick layer of mud."

Later on Allen would record the temperature of the mud as forty-five degrees.

"Want me to get started?"

Allen nodded. In a moment the squeak of rusted pulleys filled his ears as the creatures from the well were brought slowly to the surface. They glistened black and shiny from the mud and they were, Allen assumed, quite dead. After all, they had been buried for at least two decades.

"Toads?" came the question.

"Yes, indeed," said Allen. "Quite a few. I wonder how many more are down there."

And then it seemed to happen in the briefest instant of time. Six, eight, twelve legs, lifeless only a second before, had begun to twitch.

"Oh, my God! Saints preserve us!" gasped one of the men. "What is that?"

Allen bent over the toads and could just make out the faintest trace of respiration. The toads were coming to life.

No one moved or said a word. Eyes wide, mouths agape, Allen and the other men watched as the toads slowly emerged to wakefulness from their long, strange slumber. Like sleepers climbing out of a dream, they opened and closed and opened and closed their eyes, not yet seeing but far from the place they had been.

"It could not have been more than three minutes later," Allen would say, "that the toads began to move around, tentatively at first, but then with some vigor." Before long they were acting as if absolutely nothing out of the ordinary had happened.

According to *Scientific American,* Allen believed that the toads had been plunged into this curious state because of the uniformity of the mud environment; the temperature at the bottom of the well was constant, and the animals were undisturbed. Allen further added that there was no reason why the toads could not have remained that way indefinitely, poised somewhere between life and death.

While this may not be exactly the same thing as an Egyptian pharaoh returning to life after having had most of his major organs removed, being wrapped in miles of linen and stuffed in an airtight crypt for twenty-five centuries, it is, nevertheless, pretty amazing stuff. Animals—even the true hibernators—do not normally spend two decades buried in mud. But this is nothing. Animals have shown they can survive even more bizarre conditions. Take the case of "The Doctor and the Newts."

In the early 1800s, University of Cambridge geologist

Dr. Edward Clarke was fossil hunting in a quarry. At a depth of some 270 feet, Clarke discovered several excellent specimens of fossilized* sea urchins and newts (semiaquatic salamanders). Three of the newts were in quite good shape, so Clarke carefully dug them out of the rock and set them on a piece of paper. He returned to his digging, but when he checked on the newts a short time later, he almost fell over. The newts were moving!

Clarke watched goggle eyed as the newts wiggled around the paper, obviously enjoying their unexpected return to life. After a little while, though, two of the newts seemed to be slowing down, like little mechanical toys whose batteries were wearing out. But the third, oddly enough, appeared to be gaining strength, so Clarke decided to release it. He transported the newt to a pond and ceremoniously set it free.

When Clarke returned to the university with the other two newts, he learned what might be described as the punch line of the story. The three newts belonged to a species that no longer existed. The entire line had been extinct for several hundred years!

Now, meanwhile, on another continent, the rush was on for gold. Adventurers had crossed the Mississippi and Arkansas rivers and followed the Platte in search of fortunes they knew lay deep within the earth. Always exhausted, rarely successful, they chased the gold and

---

*A fossilized newt is not the same as the fossil of a newt. A fossil is an impression created in a soft material, which then hardens. When an animal is fossilized, the animal itself is preserved by a hardening process.

silver threads running through the rocks. They raised towns like Gold Point and Silver Springs and Midas and dreamed each night of finding the mother lode.

A score of prospectors were working the Lorne Lord mine. They talked mining, mostly, and about the spread they were going to buy outside Carson City. At first, no one noticed anything peculiar about the vein until the superintendent—a man named McDougal—started to soak the clay. As the water slowly seeped into the dry mud, little bits of life began to emerge. They were grubs, McDougal figured, or maybe worm larvae, three-quarters of an inch long and just barely an eighth of an inch in diameter. And they were, unquestionably, alive.

How long had the grubs been in the clay? Centuries. Perhaps longer. But even more puzzling is how the creatures were able to remain alive.

For years, scientists have ruminated over the apparent ability of animals (including, occasionally, people) to enter the strange state of cryptobiosis—literally, "hidden life"—or, as it is more commonly known, suspended animation—"withheld life." Suspended animation is not hibernation, which is a temporary, predictable condition. Animals emerge from hibernation after a specific period of time, partly in response to the onset of warmer weather and partly because their fat supplies are low. Hibernating animals, as you will recall, "bulk up" before the winter so they can sustain themselves during the long sleep. When an animal enters suspended animation, however, it is sudden and unplanned and usually in response to a dire, unforeseen emergency, such as being trapped in cooling lava. The animal has no time to prepare, but apparently it doesn't have to. It makes do with whatever stores of fat it has—if it uses them at all! While there is no doubt that hibernation increases an animal's life span, suspended animation can extend it indefinitely. Even if a hibernator were able to remain asleep much longer than usual, as soon as its life were threatened, it would wake up. An animal in suspended animation can't rouse itself; it is truly a prisoner of circumstances.

Despite what it looks like, suspended animation is not death, either. Death, by its very definition, is irreversible and damages the organism beyond repair. Instead, in suspended animation, the animal's life is held up—nature's version of the PAUSE button on your VCR. What brings the animal out? Professor Allen felt that the warm surface temperature and fresh air revived the toads from the well. For the grubs in the mine, it was as simple as adding water.

Water is also the key to reanimating a microscopic creature called a tardigrade, something that could easily be the prototype for an invader from outer space. About 85 percent of the tardigrade's total body mass is water. Remove the water and the animal goes into suspended animation. Under normal conditions, the tardigrade's life span is about a year, but dry out the animal and it can last for sixty years.

In 1972, a Soviet scientist reanimated a large number of microorganisms that had been imprisoned in a piece of potassium ore. As the scientist ran water over the ore, he noticed that bits of it were beginning to flake off and float away. Curious, he examined the flakes under a microscope and found to his absolute surprise that they were actually tiny one-celled animals and that *they had begun to reproduce!* Without question, these little creatures hold the reanimation record. When the ore was carbon-dated—tested to determine its age—it was found to be 250 million years old. The microorganisms predate the dinosaurs.

But now, however, we shall add a little twist to the riddle of suspended animation. Mystery writers who are particularly clever often like to baffle their readers with a nice, juicy locked-room mystery. A crime is committed within a room whose exits have all been sealed from the inside. Problem: How did the criminal escape? For biologists studying the puzzle of animals imprisoned in rocks and other solid objects, the challenge is not how the creatures got out, but how they got in!

The Case of the Radcliffe* Insects

In 1881, a man named John Barlow reported in the magazine *English Mechanic* a most curious state of affairs at the R. Bealey and Company Bleach and Chemical Works, Radcliffe. As two of the workers were sawing a log of

---

*Radcliffe, to establish the setting, is part of Greater Manchester in northern England. Its population is about twenty-nine thousand, and its industries include cotton mills and paper plants.

beech into planks, they cut right across a circular hole about an inch in diameter. Later, the men estimated the hole to have been located some three and one-half inches inside the original tree, the way you sometimes see air bubbles trapped within a piece of glass.

The workers finished cutting the log and began to inspect the planks, turning each one over in their survey. When they came to the plank with the hole, they noticed a fine, powdery substance, brownish in color, spill from the hole. And then, to everyone's absolute astonishment, out fell two live insects.

The workers goggled. They bent down to study the creatures and saw that they were very sluggish. Lethargic. In fact, almost asleep. Their work forgotten, the men moved the insects closer to the fire—perhaps to see better—and the warmth from the grate worked its animation magic. Gradually, the insects began to stir and move about. Had the insects been held in suspended animation?

Witnesses said the insects looked like wasps, but the wings were not quite as wide and the body was thicker. (They may have been termites, which would account for the brown powder.) Despite the wings, however, the "wasps" never did fly and probably spent the remainder of their lives inside the R. Bealey and Company Bleach and Chemical Works. But the real mystery is how the insects got into the tree in the first place since no one was able to find a passage or entrance of any kind leading to the little chamber. King Tut's tomb without the tunnel.

The Coal and the Toad—Case 1

In 1910, the British journal *Nature* told of a resident of Leicester, England's discovery of a live toad embedded in a lump of coal. When the coal was broken open, the toad appeared sluggish, but before long it was hopping around, business as usual.

> *Note: It may be of some interest to the investigator to learn that coal is formed by the extremely slow decomposition of vegetable matter under high temperatures and pressures. So how the toad got into the lump of coal may not be as nearly as remarkable as how the animal was able to survive the millennia-long process of formation!*

The Coal and the Toad—Case 2

An even better coal-and-toad story appeared in *English Mechanic* nine years earlier. A gentleman by the name of Clarke, it seems, was stirring the fire in his grate when he cracked open one of the coals with a poker. The coal had been on the fire at least an hour, according to Clarke, perhaps nearer to an hour and a half. The coal shattered and a short time later, Clarke noticed something moving in the fire. He leaned closer and saw it was a living toad. But here's the payoff. The toad was completely transparent and had no mouth!

Much to Clarke's wonderment, the toad lived over a month after its release from the coal, at which time it was put on view in Cheapside, once the site of tournaments and executions. Seems appropriate somehow.

A Trilogy of Tough Toad Cases

Case 1—The Red Sandstone

During excavations for the London and Birmingham Railway in the 1830s, workers hit a level of red sandstone* some ten feet down. As one five-inch-thick slab of sandstone was being lifted out of the site, it slipped from its ropes, crashed to the ground, and broke nearly in half. A shower of smaller fragments burst from the large slab, and a worker noticed that in one of these fragments was the imprint of a toad. As you might expect, the workers immediately forgot about the task at hand and started to search for the bottom half of the fragment. When it was finally located, what should be inside but the toad itself, fitted snug and tight like a cookie in a cookie mold.

At first the toad appeared a healthy brown color but within ten minutes had turned a rather ominous black. It also seemed to be gasping for air. But now the workers noticed that the cavity was almost the exact size and shape of the toad, and as far as they could tell, had noth-

*Sandstone is a sedimentary rock somewhat hard but easily shattered.

ing like a passage or an air tube. So they began to wonder—almost irrationally—if perhaps the fresh air was killing the toad!*

Quickly, they fitted the two sandstone halves back together again and sealed the crack with clay, but unfortunately, the toad died four days later. The cause of death remains unknown, but then again, so does the manner by which the toad got into the sandstone in the first place.

Case 2—The Iron Ore

We next come to the tale of the toad that was found in a solid block of iron ore. According to eye witnesses, the cavity in which the toad had been entombed was quite a bit larger than its prisoner and lined with carbonate of lime crystals. The presence of the crystals is really baffling, and whether they had anything to do with keeping the toad alive is anybody's guess. Like the sandstone toad, the iron ore toad also died soon after it was exposed to the air.

Case 3—The Flint

It is the year 1850, and we find workers digging a well in a rural part of France. They haul up a large slab of flint, split it in two with a pickax, and discover, to their

---

*Strange as it may sound, there are organisms on Earth that cannot live in the air. They are called anaerobic bacteria, but science has yet to find an anaerobic toad, unless, of course, we are allowed to count this one and the toad that came out of the iron ore.

absolute shock, a toad nestled deep within. According to reports, the toad was also quite shocked, but quickly gathered its wits together enough to jump out of the flint hole and start to crawl away.

Hoping, perhaps, for an encore performance, the workers snatched up the toad and returned it to its flint cavity, but this time the toad just sat there. Hmmm. Now what? A vote was taken and the workers unanimously decided to bundle up the toad along with its piece of flint and send them off to the Society of Sciences at Blois.* But the society didn't know what to do with the toad, either, so officials wrapped it up inside its little flint home in a nice, thick blanket of moss and banished it to the bowels of the subbasement.

No one checked on the toad for quite a while, but that turned out to be just fine because the toad wasn't doing much of anything, anyway. Without a food supply it wasn't eating, and the cavity in which the toad resided was clean, so the toad wasn't passing any waste products.

But here's where it gets very curious. Whenever the toad was removed from its cavity in the darkness, it just sat there, barely moving. If, however, the lights were turned on, the toad hopped away. Furthermore, if the toad was removed from the cavity and set slightly to one side of, but still on, the flint, it returned to the cavity and settled itself back inside. The scientists also noticed a tiny ledge in the cavity on which the toad rested its

---

*Blois (pronounced BLWAH') is a town in central France on the Loire River.

mouth—a kind of "jaw prop." They also saw that the bones of the toad's jaw were indented as if they had been pressing against something for a very long time. As near as anybody could tell, there was no passage, no "snorkle" through which air could pass from the outside to the center of the flint cavity. What, then, was the toad breathing? And even better, it was the unanimous opinion of the scientists who studied the toad then that the creature had been tucked away in the flint cavity for *hundreds, or perhaps thousands, of years*!

Skeptical?

You must have noticed by now that the vast majority of animals who have been found imprisoned in rocks, trees, and such are cold-blooded—frogs, toads, salamanders, newts. In fact, nowhere in the literature is there a case of, say, a bengal tiger being trapped in marble and then returning to life. That's because cold-blooded animals such as amphibians (frogs and toads) and reptiles (lizards) cannot regulate their body temperatures internally. Always, they are at the mercy of the climate, which is why you will never see a snake in the middle of the desert at high noon. Unable to adjust its internal thermostat, the snake would quickly overheat and die.

Fortunately, however, nature has provided these creatures with the ability to enter a rather remarkable state called torpor. The word comes from the Latin *torpidus*, meaning "stiff or numb." Under extremely adverse conditions, the animal is able to slow down its metabolism to such an extent that it seems almost to be dead. Toads, for instance, will burrow deep into the mud where there is virtually no air to breathe, but where the temperature is constant, as in a meat locker. There the toads will remain for perhaps years until outside conditions favor their reemergence to the world of the living.

Biologists have long known that cold-blooded animals can remain in a torpid state for exaggerated amounts of time with absolutely no indication whatsoever that their blood is circulating or that they are breathing. (Of course, *how* they are able to do this is another question entirely.) So we easily can picture a toad growing more and more languid and inactive as the temperature around it begins to fall. At fifty degrees, the toad will start to lose consciousness, and by the forty-degree mark, it will be in a state of torpor or suspended animation. This is probably what happened as the water in Professor Allen's well began to dry up leaving a layer of cool, thick mud. The toads inadvertently became trapped and went into a state of suspended animation.

But what about the toads in the flint, and the iron ore, and the sandstone? What about the toads embedded in the coal? How might an animal manage to get itself trapped in a tree trunk? Here are some suggestions:

Imagine a woodpecker working on the outer bark of a young tree. Pounding furiously in his search for insects, he gradually creates a small hole, which successive frosts further widen. After a while, there is a little cavity just barely large enough for a curious animal. The creature pushes and strains and at last manages to get inside the cavity where it soon dozes off. When it awakens, however, it discovers it is wedged in very tightly and cannot get out.

If it is autumn and the frosts come early, the animal slips into a torpid state and there it remains as the seasons melt into years. The tree grows, enlarging itself by what scientists call concentric rings, which will one day let people judge the age of the tree. The animal sleeps on, undisturbed and oblivious. Decades, even centuries hence, the tree is felled and sent downriver to the lumber mill. It is stripped of its outer bark and cut into planks. The creature is at last liberated, revived from its pseudo-death by the warmth and the fresh air. And the workers in the lumber mill think they have witnessed the impossible. . . .

From time to time, the earth returns some of its interior to the surface via volcanic explosions. The ash and steam and burning cinders burst from the throat of the mountain along with vast quantities of liquid rock. When the rock eventually cools, it becomes the glossy black-glass, obsidian, spongy-looking pumace, quartz, granite, or fine-grained basalt.

Then there is sandstone, formed, as its name suggests, from ordinary sand, sand in which a reptile or amphibian certainly can become trapped. There is also flint, a form of quartz that can trace its beginnings to the molten state. And coal, as old as the dinosaurs, born of dead plants and the action of microorganisms and then buried under sedimentary layers that turn the black goo into hard rock. In all the history of our planet, is it not possible that a few animals were buried alive in the solidifying rock? Couldn't there be travelers from another place and time imprisoned in the cliffs and mines, the trees and stones?

It was the winter of 1856. It was cold, and a thin layer of snow decorated the ground like powdered sugar. But the tunnel workers knew nothing of that, for below ground, so many meters down, the air was hot, almost stiffling. Drab, overwashed shirts glistened with sticky sweat as the men worked to complete a railway tunnel that would link the Saint Dizier and Nancy rail lines in France. Lamps flickered unsteadily, throwing eerie shapes upon the rough walls. The men squinted in the yellow half darkness.

One of the workers pointed to a massive limestone boulder. "That one there," he said.

The men raised their pickaxes, taking aim at the million-year-old rock in the name of progress. Wordlessly, they worked the limestone, swinging the heavy pickaxes until the rock began to split. The split grew wider and then suddenly the rock burst apart like some huge prehistoric egg.

And the men froze.

There was movement from the rock. Breaths held, and in an instant, a slow-motion, time-frozen instant, a massive black shape emerged from the center of the shattered rock. The creature-monster-thing slowly unfolded two huge wings, like a leathery Dracula cape that rustled in the still, heavy air of the tunnel.

No one moved. No one even blinked.

The creature staggered forward and issued a deep, throaty squawk that echoed off the rocky walls. It was a cry of birth, perhaps, and of death, for a moment later, the thing from the rock folded, slipped, collapsed like a pile of rags and died, not a meter from the men's feet.

They sent the creature-monster-thing to the small town of Gray where scientists tested and measured it and rubbed their chins in perplexity. It had a wingspan of ten feet seven inches. Its forelegs were joined to its body by membranes, like a bat's, and its leathery skin was black and oily. It had no feet, but talons instead, long and curved and decidedly sharp. Its teeth were huge and pointed.

It did not take the scientists long to identify the creature. They had, in fact, seen it many times before, but never alive, always in pictures, in books on paleontology. A pterodactyl, they said it was, a great flying reptile that existed during the Mesozoic era 160 million years ago. A dinosaur.

The *Illustrated London News* carried this remarkable story in its February 9, 1856, edition. Was it true? Or did the paper exaggerate, highlight facts that would make a juicy story? It was reported that the rock from which the pterodactyl was said to have emerged contained a molded cavity that fitted to the creature exactly. It would be excellent proof that the whole thing occurred just as the tunnel workers said, but the rock's whereabouts today are unknown.

Could a pterodactyl have survived entombed in a rock for 160 million years? Until recently, nearly all scientists believed that the dinosaurs were reptiles. Now there is some doubt. New evidence seems to suggest that the dinosaurs were warm-blooded, possibly related to birds. So if the pteradactyl-in-the-rock story is true, then it would mean a warm-blooded animal was able to enter a state of suspended animation.

Author and professor of clinical neurology at the Albert Einstein College of Medicine in New York, Oliver Sacks, tells an extraordinary story in the February 1988 issue of *Discover* magazine. In 1957, while studying with Dr. Richard Asher in London, Sacks witnessed what might arguably be called Dr. Asher's most fascinating patient. Sacks's incredible-but-true tale is retold here.

They called him Uncle Toby. He sat silent and unmoving in a large armchair beside the grandfather clock. He had been that way for seven years.

The family laundered his clothes and attended to his toilette. They tried to give him nourishment, but of course he wouldn't take it; he did not even acknowledge their presence, although he surely loved them very much. They changed his shoes and adjusted his position. It was the only movement Uncle Toby ever made.

At last they sent Uncle Toby to the hospital. His body temperature, said the doctors, was sixty-eight degrees. His thyroid had stopped functioning. His metabolism was zero. Uncle Toby was, said the doctors and nurses and specialists and technicians, in cold storage. He had entered a state of suspended animation.

So they set about warming up Uncle Toby. It took a week to raise his temperature to seventy-two degrees. It was three weeks before he could talk, but his voice was like a rusty hinge on a door that had long been sealed.

"Where am I?" Uncle Toby wanted to know. "Was I asleep?"

Uncle Toby never learned the extraordinary facts of his strange sleep. Faced with a virulent form of lung cancer, Uncle Toby's body had fought valiantly to preserve itself. Gradually, day by day, it had put itself on hold. It had slowed the muscle that was its heart and chilled the organs that made it run. It had stopped its metabolism. It would not allow itself to die of cancer. It would simply wait.

But the doctors revived Uncle Toby in their stainless-steel building, and the cancer, too, came to life. A few days later, Uncle Toby died.

Uncle Toby was, of course, a warm-blooded animal.

CHAPTER 8

Where Have All the Monsters Gone?

They stand in the Great Hall in the Museum of Natural History, overlooking the highest form of life on earth. Sometimes plaster replaces their bones, and wires hold their massive rib cages together. Their flesh is gone, long ago rotted to atoms in the ground of a prehistoric planet. Their eyes are bony sockets, hollow, like the craters on the moon. Once they stood taller than the trees and thundered over the land in unchallenged majesty. They survived each other. And then they were gone.

No animal has captured our imagination as have the dinosaurs. They were, without question, the most successful species in the history of the earth, outlasting humans by many, many millennia. The dinosaurs walked the earth for 160 million years before something wiped them out. And ever since the first monstrous skeleton was discovered in the rock, scientists have been almost obsessed with finding out just what that something was.

One early theory suggested that the dinosaurs perished because they ran out of food. Most dinosaurs appear to have been plant eaters, and their continual feeding eventually would have laid waste to much of the vegetation. With the dying off of plant eaters, their predators, the carnivores, such as *Tyrannosaurus rex,* also would have lost their food supply. Exit: the entire species.

But the theory does not hold up. It suggests that 1) the earth was completely overrun with dinosaurs, which was certainly not the case. Starvation and disease would have limited the population just as it keeps all species from running amok. (Remember the lemmings?) The starvation theory also presupposed that 2) all dinosaurs were gigantic, with gigantic appetites that were never satisfied. This is not true, either. If you have visited a museum and seen the skeletons of *Tyrannosaurus rex* and *Brontosaurus,* you might naturally be led to think that big was the order of the day. But the fact is, the vast majority of dinosaurs were quite modest in size, and some were downright tiny. As a matter of fact, not far from the dinosaurs in the American Museum of Natural History in New York is a model of the largest animal that the earth has ever known. It is the blue whale. The blue whale eats krill and microscopic organisms called plankton, but it neither feeds constantly nor scoops up everything in sight. So it seems highly unlikely that the dinosaurs starved to death. If the earth can feed blue whales, it surely could have fed a bunch of stegosauri.

Another theory that never made it blamed the extinction of the dinosaurs on the earth's changing climate. From a tropical not-so-paradise, a steamy swamp with massive, frightening-looking plants, the earth was evolving into a cooler and more temperate place. Some areas were even freezing over. The dinosaurs, unable to regulate their body temperature because they were reptiles, could not make the adjustment and slowly died out.

Several problems here. First, the dinosaurs did not die out gradually. The record in the rocks points to a comparatively sudden disappearance, a terrible cataclysm that occurred 65 million years ago and speedily erased not only the dinosaurs, but many other species as well. Second, there is an excellent chance that the dinosaurs were not reptiles. Recent evidence points strongly to their relationship to birds. The dinosaurs might then have been warm-blooded and quite able to control their body temperature automatically.

By the 1960s and 1970s, dinosaur-extinction theories began to get more colorful. Somewhat offbeat was the warm-weather-cold-weather-sex-change theory, which suggested that the sex of the dinosaurs was determined by the climate. Low temperatures produced females while high temperatures produced males. Studies have shown that this is precisely what happens to the eggs of the American alligator. If the nest temperature is held below eighty-six degrees Fahrenheit, all the hatchlings are female. A constant temperature above ninety-three degrees and the entire brood is male.

Now, in any given year, a fairly even mix of male and female dinosaurs would have been born. During the Mesozoic era earth had a decidedly tropical climate—warm and steamy—but there were temperature fluctuations, just as there are today in places like the Amazon and Equatorial Africa. In addition, the parents could have influenced the temperature of the nests by either sitting on the eggs or insulating the nests with stones, twigs, and other materials.

But let us suppose that the climate gradually began to change. The days and nights grew cooler. Temperatures plunged into the sixties, fifties, and below during several "months" of the year. Even the most doting parents could not keep the eggs warm enough.

The chilly years pass and more and more females are produced. The older males die out, and in the space of a single generation, the entire population has become female. Without mates, the species becomes extinct.

The sex-change theory is certainly clever, but like its predecessors, it has a few problems. If you assume that the dinosaurs were reptiles, then the problem is alligators. It is the alligators who have shown us how climate affects the sex of the offspring. Alligators are a very old class of animals, so if there had been a major temperature change during the Mesozoic, why didn't it wipe out the alligators? Why didn't it kill off the turtles and crocodiles? If, however, you subscribe to the idea that the dinosaurs were birds, then the theory won't work because temperature does not seem to affect the sex of developing bird embryos.

So we move on. Next is the theory that size killed the dinosaurs. They were simply too big to survive, although this didn't seem to bother them for 160 million years. Furthermore, size alone seems to have little, if any, effect on species success. The best evidence is the existence of the whale.

On the very fringes lies the suggestion that the dinosaurs died out because of chronic diarrhea. This may seem funny, but diarrhea certainly can kill if left untreated. The animal becomes severely dehydrated, the kidneys fail, and death results. But the diarrhea theory implies a specific cause, such as a parasite or a viral agent. Something had to have been introduced to account for a radical change after 160 million years, and so far, there is no evidence for it.

By the close of the 1970s, science was pretty much right where it had been a century before with regard to the great dinosaur question. The debates raged, more and more bones and eggs were unearthed, but paleontologists were no closer to solving the 65 million-year-old riddle.

The decade turned, and quietly, Nobel Prize-winning physicist Luis Alvarez and his son Walter, a geologist at the University of California, were making a rather extraordinary discovery. Their team was in the field, working at a site with a layer of rock deposited during the Cretaceous period and marking the end of the reign of dinosaurs.

The Alvarezes noticed something extremely curious about the clay in this layer. It was very rich in an element called iridium. Iridium is a silvery white metal related to platinum, but unlike platinum—which is only scarce— iridium is downright rare. Where did all this iridium come from?

Luis Alvarez knew that certain kinds of asteroids contain relatively large amounts of iridium. Sometimes these asteroids break from the pack and fall to earth as meteors. So Alvarez suggested that perhaps an iridium-rich meteor had struck the earth toward the end of the Cretaceous period. The meteor exploded on impact, dumping its iridium into the atmosphere. When the element finally settled out, it mixed with the clay and eventually was covered over by subsequent layers of sedimentary rock.

Alvarez went on to say that this meteor was not a pebble, either—not even a large boulder. To account for so much iridium, the meteor would have had to have measured some six miles across. Next time you are in a car, clock six miles on the odometer. At a steady speed of thirty miles an hour, it will take you about ten minutes to cover six miles. That's a lot. So now try to imagine a solid object, over which it would take you ten minutes to drive, striking the earth at a speed of, say, fifty-four thousand miles an hour. You can't imagine it?

Here's some help. For openers, the meteor is going to gouge out one mighty big hole in the ground.

Just outside of Winslow, Arizona, you can see the handiwork of an ordinary-size meteor. It is the famous Barrington crater. With a diameter of nearly a mile, it is quite a sight from the air. Over the years, scientists have recovered about thirty tons of material from the original meteor from as far as six miles away. When the object hit, it blasted a crater six hundred feet deep, deep enough to swallow a sixty-story office building.

The Barringer crater is certainly impressive, but it is only a dent compared to what Alvarez believes was produced when his Cretaceous meteor hit. Alvarez and the team calculate that their six-mile-long meteorite* would have produced a crater one hundred eighty miles in diameter. This is large enough to wipe out the entire state of Virginia.

Well, that certainly sounds cataclysmic enough, but could such a thing actually have happened?

Scientists have identified at least eight major meteorite impact sites, and there is strong evidence for some fifty more. Erosion and other natural forces have erased signs of the older craters, but a fair number are still visible and quite impressive. The Wolf Creek crater in West Australia has a depth of more than 160 feet. Ontario, Canada, boasts the spectacular Brent crater, which is estimated to

---

*So you don't go nuts from what appears to be very confusing meteor terminology, here is a little reference guide: A meteor is called a meteorite when it strikes the ground. As long as it's falling, it is still a meteor.

be about 500 million years old. Although sedimentation through the eons has filled it in, you can imagine what the crater must have looked like when it was fresh. The crater's diameter is nearly two miles. What a depth it must have had!

Scientists estimate that a meteor the size Alvarez had in mind strikes the earth every 100 million years on the average. If this sounds like something slightly short of eternity, it is only because you are thinking like a human instead of a 4.5 billion-year-old planet. Since its formation, Earth has been walloped by an Alvarez-type megameteorite some forty-five to fifty times, which puts this entire scenario well within the realm of possibility.

But the dinosaurs were surely not killed by a bop on the head, nor did they fall into the crater and break their necks. There had to be more.

Thanks to physics, there is a lot more, and it has to do with the mechanics of solid bodies and kinetic energy. Kinetic energy is the energy of motion; any object that is traveling has a certain amount of kinetic energy. (*Kinetic* means "moving" in Greek.) Now, logically, the more mass an object has and the faster it is speeding along, the greater its kinetic energy, and the more powerful the impact when the object comes to a stop.

Alvarez's megameteor, then, would have packed quite a wallop, based on both its staggering size and the speed at which it probably was shooting through the atmosphere. True, friction would have slowed it somewhat, but not enough to prevent it from releasing an almost mind-boggling amount of energy in a sudden and cata-strophic explosion. But even worse would have been the aftereffects.

It is 65 million years ago, and the earth is a science-fiction place, steamy and hot and covered with lush plants that creak and rustle in the gasping air. There are no lions, no tigers, no great elephants. The only mammals scam-per about on short little legs struggling to endure in a hostile world.

From a thicket of strange, fleshy trees emerges the massive outline of Brontosaurus, a lumbering, plodding mountain of an animal ponderously dragging its bulk through the swamp. Its puny head, ridiculous atop a long, undulating neck, contains barely enough brain to control its movements. Brontosaurus stops to feed, pull-ing at the giant ferns, and then moves on. A pterodactyl screeches insanely overhead, and for a second its mas-sive, leathery wings eclipse the sun. In the background, Tyrannosaurus rex rips at the still warm flesh of a lesser dinosaur, the loser in the battle to survive.

From somewhere far, far away, a great clock ticks off the minutes until death. . . .

The meteor moves through space in silent passage. It is a piece of debris, of solar-system junk, but it careers earthward like a powerful ballistic missile.

Brontosaurus blinks sleepily in the deep afternoon haze. Tyrannosaurus rex pokes after the rich internal organs of its victim. The pterodactyl shrieks and flies off toward a destination it will never reach.

The meteor plunges to Earth.

In less than a second, the Mesozoic world explodes. The impacting meteor releases a staggering amount of energy that is seen and heard and felt all around the planet. The air roars. The seas rise. The skies pulse in a blinding flash of light. At ground zero everything is incinerated in the furious heat. The rocks and soil are crushed, fused into glass and then melted. A mile away, Allosaurus lifts its head in dulled shock as a great wall of noise pushes outward from the impact site.

A gray mushroom cloud swells in eerie slow motion, squirming up through the heavy, meteor-blasted air, bulging, forming itself into a strangely benign-looking shape. Allosaurus blinks and returns to its feeding.

All at once there is a rush of flame, and a pillar of fire, like a colossal blowtorch, roars upward. The fire coils and uncoils, spinning and spiraling as it reaches for the sky.

And then the darkness, deep and silent, spreads across the place that is planet Earth.

And then the death.

Earth lies wrapped in a shadowy cocoon. The sun's rays struggle to penetrate the thick haze, but its life-giving energy is lost in the fog. Without sunlight, plants can no longer make the carbohydrates they need for life, and they slowly begin to die. This creates a deadly chain reaction that affects the animals. Animals depend almost exclusively on green plants for the manufacture of oxygen in a process called photosynthesis. In photosynthesis, green plants sweep up the carbon dioxide expelled by the animals and replace it with oxygen, a by-product in the manufacture of plant carbohydrates. So with the plants gone, the whole food chain snaps. One after the other, animals perish. The great reptiles, successful for thousands of millennia, dwindle in numbers and finally die out all together. The fliers, swimmers, crawlers, and climbers, the bottom dwellers and the scaly creatures that crept through the ooze—the ones that could not adapt—vanish forever. When the cloud finally lifts, three-quarters of Earth's plant and animal species are gone, totally wiped out. The dinosaurs have become dust and memories.

The Alvarez theory shook things up quite a bit, and within a few years of its publication, outer space cataclysms to explain the extinction of the dinosaurs became something of a fad. In 1983, paleontologists from the University of Chicago announced that they had found a curious pattern in the rocks. The geology seemed to suggest that extinctions occur on a periodic basis. Every 26 million years or so, large numbers of species suddenly die out. This kind of mass death would not be likely to occur because of illness or genetics. It's simply too regular. So the scientists turned to the solar system, famous for its cycles and patterns and predictable movements.

Before long, the first of many comets-as-the-culprit theories was born.

Far out in space, billions of miles past the orbit of Pluto, lies a vast, frozen cloud of comets. Called the Oort cloud after the Dutch astronomer Jan Oort, this comet refrigerator is sometimes shaken up by passing stars and other cosmic travelers. The comets break free of the cloud's gravity and head inward toward the sun.

Now, most of the time, the comets serenely circle the sun like planets. Round and round they go, trapped by the sun's gravitational influence, slowly losing their flimsy matter until they disintegrate. But once in a great long while, a comet gets bumped again. Saturn is in the wrong place at the wrong time, or perhaps Jupiter and Mars are in perfect alignment, providing a double gravitational whammy. The fragile comet wobbles along its orbit, and wobbles again, and suddenly pitches headlong to Earth.

Time of impact: six hours, twenty-seven minutes, eight seconds and counting. . . .

Comets, as you probably have heard, are a lot like dirty snowballs—a little dust, a little gas, a little ice, and a tremendous amount of nothing at all. Their famous tails, which may extend millions of miles, are more space than matter. But comets pack a fantastic amount of energy, and when they hit, they are like atomic bombs.

On June 30, 1908, an extraordinary event occurred near the Tunguska River in Siberia. As near as scientists can tell, what had probably been an Earth-grazing comet was somehow nudged off course just enough to send it careening toward Earth. The object, theorized to be the comet's head, appeared in the early morning sky as a bolide, or very bright fireball, streaking in a south-to-north direction over the Yenisei River Basin. A farmer thirty-seven miles away who was sitting on his front porch at the time reported a blinding flash of white light and an unbearable heat. "My shirt was almost burned on my body," he said.

The farmer lowered his eyes almost immediately, but the fireball had already passed. Then a second later, the man was literally thrown off the porch by a monsterous explosion. He was briefly knocked unconscious, and when he came to, he heard—and felt—a rolling wall of sound advance upon him. The sound deepened and rose, shaking his house and breaking all the windows.

At the crash site a huge column of fire roared skyward and was seen by witnesses at Kirensk, nearly 250 miles away. But strangest of all was the destruction caused by the blast. The comet head released so much energy that it virtually destroyed itself upon impact, so it left no crater. But it completely blew down all the trees for a radius of several miles, and they fell, not every which way, but outward from the center, one after the other, like a neat pile of pick-up-sticks.

Now, the Tunguska Event, as it was called, played havoc with the weather for a very long time. So much debris had been hurled into the atmosphere that flaming and colorful sky glows were seen well after twilight for many, many days following the explosion. A heavy layer of dust formed in the upper layers of the atmosphere creating pseudoclouds and a strange phenomenon called "night dawn." These were seen as far away as the United Kingdom!

There were other changes, too. The soil at the blast site was found to be highly radioactive (which prompted the rather exotic suggestion than an alien ship had exploded over Tunguska). It has not officially been determined whether the radioactivity altered the genetic structure of the vegetation, but for years after, plants in the area grew abnormally large. There were no fifty-foot dandelions, but growing things were not quite the size they should have been.

The Tunguska comet did a great deal of damage, and the fallout from the blast went on doing damage for a number of years. So now imagine (or at least try to) fifty comets striking the earth at the same time. Imagine a hundred comets, two hundred, a shower of thousands upon thousands of comets raining, and raining, and raining down upon the land for centuries.

Suddenly you have catastrophe. As countless tons of cometary material are deposited into the atmosphere, the sun dims and finally becomes obscured altogether. The temperature plummets. Glaciers form and an ice age develops. The land sits wrapped in a cocoon of ice and snow. All but the hardiest plants die, and very quickly, the animals that feed upon them. In a horrible, unstoppable chain reaction, class after phylum after species becomes extinct.

Pretty neat, but what exactly triggers this hypothetical rain of comets? And what would trigger it on a regular, 26 million-year basis?

Ever inventive, the astronomers came up with an exotic and vaguely science fictional–sounding theory. Presenting: Nemesis—The Death Star:

Once upon a time, in an observatory far, far away, astronomers learned that the sun is a bit of an oddball. It is a single sun in a universe filled with double, triple, and quadruple star systems. After studying how stars clump together, the astronomers noticed that the vast majority of stars are binary; that is, two stars are locked in a gravitational embrace. Like the end weights on a set of dumbbells, they rotate around each other. Stars, too, were often found in threes—the dumbbell configuration with the third star either circling close to one of the dumbbell stars or carving out a great elliptical path around both stars. Quads were also found. So multiple star systems are without question the standard of excellence for stars, and loners are very scarce.

Our sun is a loner.

Of course, this would be perfectly acceptable if scientists didn't have a kind of "odd man out" paranoia; they hate it when our solar system doesn't conform. So enter, stage right, the dinosaurs—or rather the mystery of their extinction. Enter, too, the theory of the periodic rain of comets. What shakes the comets loose in such huge numbers? The scientists offered Nemesis, the sun's evil twin.

According to the theory, Nemesis is a dark star, perhaps a brown dwarf or the burned-out corpse of a star. This explains why Nemesis has not yet been detected by optical telescopes. Nemesis is extremely far away, well past the Oort cloud, so it is bound only very loosely to the sun by gravity. (The farther away two objects are from each other, the weaker their gravitational attraction.) As Nemesis and the sun slowly advance through their orbit, Nemesis, because of where it is positioned, periodically passes through the Oort cloud.* Every 26 million years, Nemesis' gravity disturbs the comets, dragging them out of the cloud and sending them hurtling toward Earth.

But Nemesis, says Piet Hut of the Institute for Advanced Study at Princeton, is not very likely to exist. Hut has calculated that Nemesis would have to be some 2.5 light-years from Earth to put it on track for an Oort cloud passage. At this distance (about 14 trillion miles), the gravitational attraction between the two stars would be so weak that Nemesis would have drifted or been pulled away long ago. So the Nemesis theory, although exciting and exotic, is done in by simple physics.

---

*Imagine yourself on your bike riding around the outdoor track at the local high school. Somewhere along the track there is a big puddle. If you maintain a steady speed, you will splash through the puddle at exact intervals—say, every three minutes—as you pedal around the track. In this example, the puddle is the Oort cloud and you are Nemesis.

Similar but equally doomed is the Planet X theory. Planet X is said to lie far outside the orbit of Pluto. It follows a highly elliptical orbit, something that looks like a stretched-out rubber band or the string you use when you play cat's cradle. Planet X must have a long and lanky orbit to take it through the Oort cloud. The Oort cloud is believed to lie between 3 trillion and 9 trillion miles from the sun. This is about halfway to the nearest star system, Alpha Centauri. So Planet X really reaches far into space to make its pass through the Oort cloud.

Now, each time Planet X plows into the cloud, it stirs up the comets and sends them raining down upon the earth. According to the theory, this should be once every 26 million years. But if Planet X only makes the cloud once in 26 million years, it has an orbit that is impossibly slow.

The great scientist Johannes Kepler worked out the speed at which planets must travel around the sun (and all stars, for that matter). This is one of Kepler's Laws of Planetary Motion, and there is no fudging or fooling with it. So if Planet X is really a planet, it has to follow the rules of the road and move around the sun at a specified pace. If it crosses the Oort cloud only once in 26 million years, it is breaking Kepler's law. But if it follows Kepler's law, it has to cross the Oort cloud much more often.

Now we've got a problem. Since Planet X causes a rain of comets every time it enters the Oort cloud, and if it enters the Oort cloud more frequently than once in every 26 million years, the earth is going to have to see an awful lot of comet rains. And because each of these comet rains lasts for hundreds and perhaps thousands of years, as soon as one of them ends another begins, because by that time Planet X will have entered the Oort cloud again!

Very obviously, it is not raining comets, and it is this little detail that spells the demise of the Planet X theory of dinosaur extinction.

So what are we left with? Which theory has been tough enough to run the gauntlet of scrutiny and emerge as the solution to one of nature's greatest mysteries?

None.

The secret is still safe.

CHAPTER 9

Wildman of the Woods

There is something out there, deep among the tall pines of the Pacific Northwest. It is nocturnal, foraging for roots and berries, nuts, and an occasional bit of meat under the generous cloak of darkness. It leaves tracks.

There is something out there, moving across the frozen snow of the Himalayas. It is stooped and shaggy, and its cone-shaped head seems almost too small for its great bulk. The Sherpas call it *metoh-kangmi*. It leaves tracks.

There is something out there, appearing and disappearing in the dense South American rain forest. It walks upright, like a human, through the oppressive heat, the tangled, choking plant life, the ropy lianas that hang from the trees like streamers. The Indians have

A Bigfoot by Any Other Name. . . .

Bigfoot—Anglo-American name coined by the press in the 1920s

Sasquatch—a Salish Indian name meaning "wild man of the woods"; used mostly in Canada

Oh-mah-'ah, or in its shorter form, **Ohma**—used by the Hupa Indian tribe of the Klamath Mountains of northern California

Seeahtik—used in the northern Cascades for the creature that inhabits Vancouver Island

Toki-mussi, gilyuk, hoquiam—used by the tribes in the Pacific Northwest and northern California

In the Himalayas, a Bigfoot-like creature is called:

yeti

rakshas—occasionally used in the northern part of Nepal; it is a Sanskrit word for "demon"

metoh-kangmi—a Tibetan phrase meaning "Abominable Snowman"

Jungli-admi or **Songpa**—from Sikkim, a south-central region of Asia in the Himalayas, although the words probably refer to true humans rather than to the yeti

In South America, a kind of half-man, half-ape creature is called:

mapinguary, capelobo, pelobo—from the tribes in the south, across the Amazon Delta, and into the country of Brazil

di-di or **Mono Grande,** meaning, "great monkey"—used throughout Equador, Colombia, and Venezuela

seen it, but only rarely. They tell stories that white men don't believe, of the *pelobo*, the *Mono Grande*. It leaves tracks.

This is the story of three creatures that science has not yet found. They are known by dozens of different names—Sasquatch, yeti, *capelobo*, *Oh-mah-'ah*, Bigfoot, the Abominable Snowman. For years, for decades, the creatures were nothing more than legends, but as we chop back the jungle and cut roads into the Pacific wilderness, the legends have started to come to life. To date, there have been well over fifteen hundred Bigfoot sightings throughout the United States and Canada. Yeti has been spotted across Pakistan and Nepal, and unusual fossil remains have been unearthed in Pakistan. Reports of *Mono Grande*, the "great monkey," trickle out of Brazil, Equador, Venezuela, Guyana. The descriptions are eerily consistent—apelike, but not an ape; humanlike, but not a human. It stands erect and walks on two legs, slogging through the mud, over hard-packed snow, and giving us only fleeting signs of its passage. Something is definitely out there, and time and again it leaves tracks.

The very first Bigfoot stories carried into "civilization" by hunters and other outdoorsy types probably had little effect. When America was new and rich with unexplored land, a creature from the forest was perfectly plausible. After all, the *Mayflower* people had encountered naked, feather-bedecked "savages" when they disembarked. The savages had dark skin, painted their bodies, and spoke a language that bore not the remotest resemblance to English. Some place this America was! Of course there were probably big hairy monsters running around in the woods.

But as we became more learned, more full of ourselves, we failed to swallow the Bigfoot stories anymore. The argument went something like this:

"Oh, gimme a break! If there was something out there, we woulda found it by now. We woulda captured a Bigfoot. We woulda at least gotten a picture of the thing. How come there's no hard proof, huh? How come none of them trappers and hunters ever shot one?"

And so, Bigfoot and its Canadian counterpart, Sasquatch, quickly lost credibility even though the reports continued to come in. The scientific community issued a directive: "Bring one back—dead or alive—and we'll believe."

So out they went to bag a Bigfoot.

In 1884, there was a brief flutter of activity in British Columbia when a group of trainmen captured what was billed as a young Sasquatch. The creature stood four foot seven, weighed 127 pounds, had short, glossy hair, and two extremely long arms. The trainmen named the creature Jacko.

But Jacko didn't hang around for very long and escaped at the first available opportunity. It was probably just as well. His size and coloring, his slumped shoulders and long, dangling arms suggest a run-of-the-mill chimpanzee. But why, you might be wondering, didn't the trainmen know that? A chimpanzee is hardly an exotic animal.

The year, remember, was 1884 and the place, a rather remote spot along the Fraser River in western Canada. Chimpanzees are native to Africa, not Canada, and at the time they were extremely rare in zoos. So there is an excellent chance that the trainmen had never seen one. Furthermore, Bigfoot's physical description was hardly a government secret. If people didn't know the specifics of its height, weight, and shoe size, they did know that Bigfoot was a "hairy ape-man" of considerable strength. So it is more than likely that the trainmen reported seeing what they wanted to see. The press, of course, did the rest, and the Jacko story has persisted to this day as an eyewitness account.

The sightings continued, but the mighty Bigfoot/Sasquatch hunters had little, if any, opportunity to fire a single shot at the ellusive brute.

"But he's out there!" they insisted. "I seen them tracks, bigger'n you kin imagine!"

A number of quick thinkers produced plaster casts, many of which were so phony the scientists didn't even have to bother studying them with a magnifying glass to see details. Other tracks were clearly those of bears. The prints had been made in the snow, which, after a warm spell, had melted a little, thereby enlarging and distorting the impressions. And then there were a few rather curious seventeen-inch-long humanlike footprints that absolutely no one in the scientific community wanted anything to do with. They couldn't be classified, identified, or recognized. Very odd, indeed. It was best, judged the scientists, to leave them alone. . . .

But just when things were beginning to get boring, a man named Albert Ostman returned from the head of Toba Inlet in British Columbia with a whopper of a Sasquatch report. No, Ostman did not have a specimen tucked away in his knapsack; what he had was the hair-raising, spine-tingling tale of his own kidnapping.

WARNING!

EYEWITNESS REPORTS,

NO MATTER HOW RELIABLE THE SOURCE,

SHOULD NOT BE USED AS EVIDENCE THAT BIGFOOT EXISTS

Albert Ostman, a retired lumberjack, was on vacation. He had chosen a remote and wildly beautiful spot along one of the many inlets rippling the coast of British Columbia. An Indian guide had taken Ostman to where he would make his first camp. He watched in silence as Ostman pitched his small tent and set out the tinned foodstuffs and eating utensils he had brought. After a while, the guide spoke.

He told of the many abandoned gold mines in the area, of the hopeful prospectors who had come and gone, and of the one who had been killed. Then the guide lowered his voice. There were, he said, strange kinds of humans in the area. They were large, much taller than a man, and covered with hair. His uncle had seen the footprints.

Almost two feet in length they were, and very broad.

Ostman may have snickered. He may have shrugged it all off as exaggeration. He may have trembled in his hiking boots. But whatever his reaction to the guide's story, he stayed where he was.

On the first day, Ostman explored his surroundings, turning over rocks and examining them with the hope of finding some interesting specimens. The guide accompanied him until twilight began to descend, at which point he bade Ostman good luck and returned (probably with some degree of relief) to the safety of civilization.

As the week unfolded, Ostman moved his camp to higher and higher ground. Before long, he had climbed about a thousand feet and pushed farther and farther into some very remote territory. But it was magnificent, this part of Canada, and Ostman gave little thought to the guide's words.

Ostman at last settled down beside a small stream that looked out to a thick grove of cypress trees. After a modest dinner from his supplies of tinned and dehydrated food, Ostman unrolled his sleeping bag and crawled in. The night was refreshingly cool, and the cypress trees swayed gently in the deep silence. Ostman was asleep almost at once.

The following day passed uneventfully, but the following night most certainly did not. In fact, according to Ostman, he had the wilderness adventure of a lifetime, escaping with his life only by sheer luck.

Ostman lay curled in his sleeping bag, his campfire little more than faintly glowing embers. His breathing was smooth and regular. Silver stars blinked through the swaying trees. It was the perfect picture of primeval peace. And then suddenly, Ostman was shaken from sleep. He had slid or been crammed into the bottom of his sleeping bag like a bunch of potatoes and was, he judged, several feet off the ground.

Ostman looked up and saw to his horror an enormous hairy fist clutching the open end of his sleeping bag. Helpless and growing increasingly uncomfortable with each passing minute, Ostman bumped and bounced over very rough terrain for perhaps twenty miles (Ostman's estimate). Finally he was deposited, much like the bag of aforementioned potatoes, on the hard ground.

Ostman's legs were cramped and numb, and it took some time before the feeling returned, but he managed to crawl with some difficulty from the depths of his sleeping bag. As he had been in the dark for about three hours, Ostman could see quite clearly the improbable scene before him. There in the thin light of the approaching dawn stood four Sasquatch—father (Ostman's kidnapper), mother, and two children.

Ostman then describes his Sasquatch family in great detail. The son, he says, was between eleven and eighteen years old, although it is unclear whether Ostman was going by human or primate standards. His chest measured between fifty and fifty-five inches and his waist was about a thirty-eight. The father was proportionately larger—eight feet tall with about a thirty-inch neck.

In all, Ostman claims to have spent six days in Sasquatch captivity, able to move freely about but "stopped at the border," so to speak, when he tried to wander too far away. The Sasquatch did nothing whatsoever to harm Ostman or even interfere with his movements. They seemed, instead, to be studying him and were particularly fascinated by his little tin of snuff.* This, eventually, gave Ostman his opportunity for escape.

As Ostman tells it, he had just used a little bit of snuff when the father Sasquatch leaned forward and snatched the tin from his hand. Then, before Ostman could stop him (although how he could have done this is anybody's guess), the Sasquatch gulped down the entire contents of the container. The Sasquatch's reaction was immediate and violent, and the animal fell to the ground writhing in pain. Timing is everything, they say, and the minute the attention was diverted to father Sasquatch, Ostman took his leave.

Ostman's alleged kidnapping occurred in 1924, but Ostman did not breathe a word of it until thirty-three years later. Then, in August of 1957, he formally declared the truth of his story in front of a justice of the peace in British Columbia. Ostman's reason for keeping silent was the fear of ridicule, which the time lapse did

*Snuff is a lot like chewing tobacco, although it was often sniffed.

little to prevent. When Ostman finally went public, he had his share of hecklers.

Ostman's story cannot be proved. Ostman brought nothing back with him from the Sasquatch camp, and of course there are no photographs. While his descriptions of the Sasquatch are perfectly plausible, they could have been lifted from books and newspaper articles. He sheds absolutely no light on the behavior and habits of the Sasquatch despite the fact that he spent six full days with the creatures. But most suspect of all is Ostman's description of the Sasquatch diet: grasses, roots, spruce and hemlock tips, and tubers. According to anthropologist John Napier, this is not nearly enough to sustain an animal the size of Sasquatch. Even if the animals continually gathered and ate and gathered and ate (which they did not, according to Ostman), it is doubtful that this extremely limited vegetarian diet would be sufficient.

But if this was all a hoax—or at least a tall tale—why did Ostman wait thirty years before he told it? Well, who says he waited thirty years? He might have come up with the idea in 1957 and used his old 1924 camping trip as the setting.

Ostman's story—true or not—was a stick of dynamite. It shook up the Bigfoot believers and sent them scrambling into the forests of the Pacific Northwest. Expeditions, all supported by private funds, were organized and launched, but nothing really good happened until 1967. That's when Roger Patterson made his home movie.

It was autumn in Bigfoot country. Roger Patterson

reined up his horse and slowly scanned the tree-thick landscape. Up here in the cool Bluff Creek Valley of northern California, it would be easy to hide a race of hairy giants. For miles, everywhere you looked there was nothing but mountains and deep green forest. Much of it was government land, and much of it was remote and untracked. Patterson nodded. *Real easy,* he thought, *for Bigfoot to hide.*

Patterson had dabbled in show business for a while and had worked the rodeo circuit before getting interested in Bigfoot. But his interest quickly grew into a passion, and Patterson soon turned all his attention to tracking the creature. He established the Northwest Research Foundation for collecting data on sightings, footprints, and other evidence. And of course, Patterson went on expeditions.

The 1967 expedition to Bluff Creek Valley began uneventfully. Patterson and his colleague Bob Grimlin had been receiving reports of scattered sightings and footprints in the area, and they were anxious to check them out. Naturally, they hoped for a sighting themselves, but the region is heavily forested and vast, and in the Bigfoot game of hide-and-seek, luck is everything.

Patterson and Grimlin had been riding through the high country, not saying much and finding even less, when all of a sudden, Patterson spotted something in the trees. He knew immediately, and his heartbeat nearly doubled. It was, he would determine later, a female Bigfoot, heavily built and covered with short, reddish dark hair. She peered at Patterson, or perhaps at nothing at all, without the slightest concern, almost nonchalantly. Patterson, on the other hand, went nuts. In a split second, he was off his horse, camera aimed and running, capturing a living "something-or-other" on 16mm color film.

Patterson shot about twenty feet of film before the creature disappeared into the thick trees. The picture is reasonably well focused, but it is understandably jerky; Patterson was just a tad excited. It shows a muscular, hairy, two-legged animal with features that are curiously both human and apelike. For instance, apes and other primates do not walk erect; their weight distribution and center of gravity are very different from a human's. Roger Patterson's animal walks erect. Apes and primates do not have necks. Instead, their heads sit squarely on their shoulders, giving them a hunched look. Roger Patterson's animal doesn't have a neck.

One physiological characteristic of our upright stance is our gluteus maximus, or buttocks muscles. These well-developed muscles balance us so we can stand up. Apes, gorillas, and the rest of the primates do not have buttocks, but Patterson's animal does.

So the creature seems to be some sort of composite. Its upper body suggests an ape, its lower body a human. But this description is a little scary to scientists. It smacks of myths and legends and imaginary beasts. Patterson's animal seems too fantastic to be real, and so, concluded most scientists, the film must therefore be a fake. Patterson either built the creature or "created" it by having someone don a gorilla suit and stomp around through the trees.

Then there was the issue of film speed. Patterson's camera was capable of shooting at either sixteen or twenty-four frames per second, but Patterson said he could not remember at what speed he took the pictures. If Patterson shot twenty-four frames a second, the creature's gait is decidedly human, but at sixteen frames per second, the animal shows some very unhumanlike walking patterns.

Patterson's film was shown to the special-effects technicians who had built the original King Kong for the movies. The technicians watched with mounting interest, fascinated by the strange, hulking creature. Could they make the animal shown in the film? they were asked. Would it be possible? The technicians shook their heads. Despite their talent, their experience and resources, they very much doubted it. Certainly they could try, they said, but they "would have to create a completely new system of artificial muscles and find an actor who could be trained to walk like [the animal in Patterson's film]." The technicians shrugged. "It might be done, but we would have to say that it would be almost impossible."

Next came Don Grieve, a lecturer in biomechanics at the Royal Free Hospital in London. Grieve stated that if the film had been shot at twenty-four frames per second, the "animal" could have been an actor, but Grieve brought up a very interesting point. In order to create the illusion of bulk, the actor would have to be heavily padded. (Patterson's animal is estimated to weigh about 350 pounds.) But even the best padding has its limits. Because it is only cotton wool and foam rubber, latex and cloth, it doesn't respond to movement the way real muscle and fat would. It is going to crease and bunch in funny, unnatural ways, not to mention severely restrict the person's actions.

Anthropologist John Napier saw the Patterson film in 1967 and in his opinion, the creature's walk seems "self-conscious. The swing of the arms and legs," he said, "was grossly exaggerated."

To further confuse the issue, Patterson produced casts of footprints, which he claimed had been made by the creature in the film. The prints measure 14½ inches long and correspond to an animal standing 6½ to 7 feet high. Admittedly, this is well within the range for humans, but it is also well within the range for Bigfoot. You will hear that most estimates put Bigfoot at upward of 8 feet tall; however, that is an adult male Bigfoot, a Bigfoot that has reached its maximum height. Aren't there any juvenile Bigfoot? Doesn't Bigfoot—if it exists at all—start out small, just like us? Just like all living things? Somewhere along the line, wouldn't Bigfoot have to pass through the 6-foot mark on its way to its full-grown height?

It has been more than twenty years since Roger Patterson took his famous home movie, and science still is unable to prove him a fraud or a genuine eyewitness.

We probably will never know the truth, but Patterson's film certainly changed things. No other account or story, no physical evidence had ever stirred so much controversy and cast so much doubt. While the great majority of scientists still insisted that Bigfoot did not and could not exist, some began to have second thoughts. Gradually, anthropologists such as Oxford University's Myra Shackley and Washington State University's Grover Krantz found themselves wondering if it could be possible. . . .

"I didn't put much likelihood into this creature being real," writes Krantz, "until the spring of 1970." That's when Krantz got hold of some rather extraordinary plaster casts. The casts show an enormous foot, seventeen inches in length and nearly six inches in width. To appreciate this size, measure off a rectangle seventeen inches long and six inches wide on a piece of paper. (Typing paper is 8½ by 11 inches.) Now, take off your shoe and place your foot inside the rectangle. That is how your foot compares to what may very well be Bigfoot's foot.

Krantz has casts for both the right and left footprints of a single individual, but the prints do not match. They do not match because there appears to be a deformity in the right foot. There are two distinct bulges on the outside edge, which Krantz believes may have been caused by an inflammation of the cartilage. Now, this is extremely lucky, because by comparing both casts, Krantz was able to reconstruct the bones in the foot.

Krantz found—not a larger version of the human foot—but a decidedly different foot. The ankle, for example, is set farther forward, and the heel and foresection of the foot are not in the same proportion as those of a human foot. The heel is much larger, which agrees with the forward placement of the ankle. This is clearly sophisticated stuff and, Krantz believes, far beyond the capabilities and knowledge of your average Bigfoot hoaxer.

Without question, footprints comprise the bulk of the Bigfoot evidence. Many are outright fakes, the simplest of which are made in snow or soft earth with "Bigfoot shoes." Absolutely no one is fooled by these because the prints are flat and featureless, whereas a real footprint would have uneven depressions. (You know this if you ever have walked on sand with your bare feet.)

Other fake prints are what can be called "meltdowns." A meltdown footprint is made in snow by either an animal or a human but not photographed until the snow begins to melt. The melting enlarges and distorts what would be an easily recognizable print. The meltdown print has depressions and features because it is a genuine footprint, but it is much larger. At this stage of the game, though, the investigators are on to this little scam.

A large number of "Bigfoot" prints fall into the category of mistaken identity. UFO reports suffer from the same problem. Many people who claim to have come across footprints in the woods cannot tell bear tracks from raccoon tracks. When the tracks are enlarged by rain or temperature changes, an inexperienced hiker easily can jump to conclusions—especially if he or she has Bigfoot on the brain.

When you are dealing with someone like Grover Krantz, a Bigfoot print is tough to fake. Bigfoot has flat arches, large heels, short toes, and wide forefeet. Furthermore, when a real animal walks, it kicks up a little mound of dirt just behind the ball of the foot. A fake foot will kick up a mound of dirt just behind the toes because it doesn't have working muscles and cartilage.

Another detail footprint fakers would have trouble with is print depth. It stands to reason that an eight hundred-pound Bigfoot is going to leave a deeper footprint than a two hundred-pound human. It is a fairly straightforward process to compute the weight of the animal that made the tracks from the depth of the depression. You might hire four or five circus acrobats to stand on each other's shoulders so that their combined weight is eight hundred pounds, but a fake foot is still going to leave a fake footprint.

Krantz has a collection of about twenty casts that he believes are the genuine article. But the very best by far is a cast made in the summer of 1982 by Paul Freeman, a United States Forest Service patrolman in Walla Walla, Washington. This particular cast is so extraordinary, the chance of its being phony is practically zero.

It began on June 10, a Thursday. Freeman had been tracking elk along a deserted logging road when he came across the creature. Freeman froze. The creature, perhaps just as startled, also froze. The two stood there unmoving, staring at each other with a mixture of shock, awe, and curiosity. Then all at once, the creature turned and moved off into the thick trees. When Freeman returned to the site a short time later with his supervisors, they found enormous footprints. The ground was hard, but the impressions were an inch deep, evidence that whatever made them had to have been very heavy.

Freeman had described the creature as being about eight feet tall and powerfully built, and indeed, the plaster casts that were taken at the scene bore this out. They measured 14½ inches long and had been made by an animal estimated to weigh between six hundred and eight hundred pounds. The casts also showed that the creature was flat-footed, and there was a curious widening of the second toe on the left foot.

Now, as if this wasn't enough, the following week Freeman again found tracks in the same vicinity. This time the casts revealed two individuals, one of which was the creature Freeman had seen on June 10. The left foot showed the identical characteristic second toe, and the other animal's tracks indicated that it had stepped on a stone—the foot had spread out and impressed the ground on either side of the object. But even more exciting was the clear, absolutely unmistakable presence of what are called dermal ridges—toe prints.

In all higher primates, toes as well as fingers have characteristic loops and whorls, tiny swirling lines that are unique and individual. No two beings have quite the same pattern, which is why fingerprints at the scene of the crime often can be such damning evidence.

So Krantz wasted no time sending the casts off to the FBI, perhaps the best fingerprint experts in the business. The FBI agreed; yes, those were dermal ridges, all right, but no one on the staff would venture any sort of opinion about the creature that owned them.

Tim White, a paleontologist at the University of California at Berkeley said that he could not imagine how anyone could fake such a thing but added, "I have to reserve judgment until Grover [Krantz] brings me a tooth or a bone."

Krantz is understandably frustrated by the scientific community's reluctance to accept what he feels is very strong evidence, but he does admit that footprints—no matter how good—are still only circumstantial. If there are large, bipedal (two legged) primates living in the forests of the Northwest, Krantz knows he will have to produce one—dead or alive. But this could create other problems.

Officially, Bigfoot doesn't exist. At best, it is considered a hypothetical creature sighted from time to time and frequently the subject of faked evidence and hoaxes. But curiously, in some parts of the country, this phony monster is protected by law.

In 1969, Skamania County in Oregon adopted Ordinance 69–01 prohibiting the hunting of Bigfoot. Beginning April 1 of that year, shooting a nonexistent Bigfoot became a felony punishable by a fine of up to ten thousand dollars and/or five years in jail. Science and the law work in mysterious ways. . . .

But what exactly it is that's being protected?

About a year after the Oregon law, a rare Bigfoot handprint was found in northern Washington State. It revealed an enormous palm, twice the size of a man's, and a thumb that is in line with the rest of the fingers. This last feature is very significant. Bigfoot does not have an opposable thumb.

All living apes—not to mention human beings—have thumbs that are set at right angles to the other fingers. This allows the thumb to bend inward so it can touch all four fingers. (Three fingers in the case of apes.) So, based on the handprint, Bigfoot is neither an ape nor a human. But the plot thickens when we consider Bigfoot's toes. Footprints clearly show a large first toe that it not opposable. In apes, the first toe is opposable; in humans, it isn't. Bigfoot's feet, then, put the creature closer to humans than to apes! But without a specimen, there is really no way to classify Bigfoot, although there have been some suggestions.

One theory says that Bigfoot is a remnant of Neanderthal man, an early race of humans that lived about 100,000 years ago. This does not seem very likely, however, because the Neanderthals were not dim-witted, hairy ape-men. Archaeological evidence has shown us that these people walked upright, made simple tools, and understood death and mourning. Furthermore, Neanderthal was much shorter than Bigfoot—an average of five foot five compared to a towering eight feet for Bigfoot.

Another suggestion classifies Bigfoot as a surviving form of the giant ape, *Gigantopithecus.* (The name means "giant ape" in Greek.) The clues we have for *Gigantopithecus* are few, indeed—only some bones and teeth—but the archaeologists have been able to recreate the animal on paper. There is a physical similarity, but *Gigantopithecus* evolved about 9 million years ago in Asia. It may have crossed into North America via a land bridge and ended up as Bigfoot. (Although if *Gigantopithecus* did not cross and did not die out, it could conceivably fill the bill for the Asian yeti.)

Finally, Bigfoot might be a giant orangutan, although the orangutan also is found exclusively in Asia. It, too, would have had to cross a land bridge and then manage to survive in what for the orangutan was a very alien climate. Interestingly enough, though, the orangutan is called "the wild man of the woods" in Southeast Asia. It is a red-haired, roly-poly sort of fellow that looks an awful lot like a man (or woman) in an ape suit. But the footprints do not match with Bigfoot's, as the orang has a very obvious opposable first toe.

So we are now out of suggestions, but as archaeologist Myra Shackley writes in her book *Still Living?*, "For me there is no question of whether [Bigfoot] exist . . . but only of how they should be classified."

But one question continues to nag: How could an eight-foot-tall primate escape detection and capture for so many years? If the thing really exists, how come no-body's nabbed it?

We ask this question because we have a pretty high opinion of ourselves. Since we are apparently the most intelligent form of life on the planet, we think we know everything.

Well, consider the following:

Everybody was absolutely certain that the coelacanth had died out more than 70 million years ago. It had been a strange, electric blue fish that dwelt in the very deepest parts of the ocean and shared the world with the great dinosaurs. Day after day, fishermen cast their nets and dropped their lines. Scuba divers descended in wet suits and diving bells and bathyscaphes. And no one ever saw the coelacanth, but it was down there all along, alive and well and nowhere near extinction.

Then we have the giant panda, as big as a bear, but not discovered until 1869. How did we overlook it? One rea-son is its extremely small population. The panda has been reduced almost to the point of extinction, so locat-ing one is a bit like looking for a needle in a haystack. In addition, the panda's territory is six thousand feet up in the dense bamboo forests of China. No wonder we missed it!

At present, there are approximately one million spe-cies of animals on the earth. Every year scientists dis-cover about eight thousand new insect species, but they believe that there are anywhere from one million to ten million species *that have not yet been found!* While an eight-foot, eight hundred-pound hairy primate is somewhat larger than a bug, it can still get lost. Bigfoot is nocturnal and shy and avoids people. It does not cook its food, so there is no smoke from a camp fire to reveal its whereabouts. When death is near, it goes off by itself like so many other animals. Unless we take teams of trackers into the mountains and scour the forests, we are not going to find any bones. Its population is estimated to be perhaps two thousand at the most.

Yes, Bigfoot could have escaped detection.

But time may be running out for Bigfoot. As we push our bulldozers and earth movers farther and farther into the wilderness, Bigfoot's territory is growing smaller. In many parts of New England, we have slowly stolen the land that once belonged to the raccoons. Now raccoons are turning up everywhere—from local parks to people's chimneys. They have no place to run. And the same may be true for Bigfoot. One day soon you will see a startling headline on the front page of every newspaper in the country:

BIGFOOT FOUND!

. . . and probably shot.

Let's hope he is out there.

Let's hope we never find him.

CHAPTER 10

Snake in the Lake

The sightings had been going on for years, but it was strictly a local affair. The townspeople were comfortable with their sea serpent and often amused by it. They took pictures only if they happened to have brought a camera to the lake along with the picnic things. Mostly, they just spotted the two or three humps by sheer chance, smiled, and then went about their business.

They called her Nessie. She was a female, they knew, but could not say why. She dwelt in the murky, almost bottomless depths of Loch Ness, feeding, perhaps, on salmon. She had been trapped, they surmised, by the last ice age when the loch was closed forever to the sea. She was prehistoric, with a long, undulating neck, a massive blimp-shaped body, and a small head crowned by two little horns, although it was hard to tell what they really were from such distances.

The good people of Loch Ness did not question or probe. They did not organize research teams with heat-seeking devices and sonar. They did not plumb the loch. Instead, they embraced Nessie with the affection one feels for a funny-looking mutt that keeps hanging around. And all was calm and serene at Loch Ness.

But then the reporters came.

The press learned of the local monster when the road that skirted the loch was rebuilt in the early 1930s. The new road could now accommodate more traffic, and as the cars began to sweep by one after the other, more and more eyes were trained on the water and more sightings reported. Also, during construction great numbers of trees and masses of shrubbery had to be brought down on the loch side of the road. This allowed for longer stretches of unobstructed viewing. Motorists and visitors could see much farther out into the loch. Finally, all the rock blasting that was done may have disturbed Nessie, driving her to the surface more frequently.*

Between 1933 and 1934, there was a rash of sightings—well over two hundred—so it is no wonder that the newspapers pounced. On May 2, 1933, the *Inverness Courier* ran the story of an unidentified, long-necked creature in the loch, and in no time at all the wire services

---

*One of Nessie's characteristics seems to be very acute hearing, and an animal that hears well invariably reacts to loud and sudden sounds.

had it. The Loch Ness monster, as it came to be called, was front-page stuff.

Reporters and tourists descended upon the Loch Ness region like a cloud of hungry locusts. They came with their cameras and binoculars, their miles of film and tripods. The new road carried chugging black roadsters crammed with visitors and overflowing with suitcases. And all eyes were trained on the dark waters of the loch, straining for a glimpse of the now-famous long neck and glistening hump.

The impassive locals took all the fuss in stride while quietly pocketing the extra money from room and boat rentals. With sublime patience, they allowed themselves to be asked the same questions over and over again: Have you seen the monster? What did it look like? What was the weather like? Did you take any pictures? Do you have any theories on what the creature is? How do you think it got into the loch? And on, and on, and on.

Alex Campbell has claimed to have seen Nessie some eighteen times in his forty years of service as a water bailiff for Loch Ness. Before he retired, he would patrol the loch often, his chief responsibility being to protect the salmon that enter the cold, yellowish waters. Campbell's first sighting occurred in the spring of 1934 when he was thirty-two years old. If he still is alive today, he probably is going for some kind of Nessie watch record.

According to Campbell, there was a sudden and violent upsurge of water about 250 yards out on the lake. Then, moments later, a long neck appeared, topped by a small, football-shaped head "that kept turning nervously," said Campbell. "Oh, the head was just going!"

Campbell blinked several times, telling himself that the strange vision was fantastic, and wondering, perhaps, if he were having a hallucination. But no, the thing seemed quite real, and so Campbell just stared. All at once, a trawler appeared. (There is a lot of traffic on the lake.) The creature must have heard it, for it turned its head in the direction of the trawler and then immediately disappeared beneath the murky waters.

The year before, George Spicer and his wife claimed to have encountered Nessie on land. They were traveling on the loch road between the villages of Dores and Foyer when they came across what they described as a huge snail inching its way down an embankment to the water's edge. They had one word for the sight: *loathsome.* Indeed!

Winifred Cary, whose home overlooks Urquhart Bay on the loch, says she first saw Nessie when she was out fishing at age eleven with her brother. "As we were going east along the pier, there suddenly rose up in the middle of the loch—not near the boat, fortunately—this colossal thing like a great whale. It was going fast against the wind and was only up for a second or two."

Mrs. Cary admits that not a soul believed her when she and her brother recounted their fantastic story, but since that day in 1917, she has seen "the beastie" fifteen times. She describes it as thirty or forty feet long—with a snakelike neck and small head.

These were the kinds of monster tales that greeted the tourists and newspaper reporters who came to Loch Ness in the 1930s. All of the tales were very consistent and curiously understated. No one made wild claims or offered unlikely descriptions. In short, the whole thing was completely believable.

In the summer of 1934, Sir Edward Mountain organized a little Nessie watch. About a dozen people stationed themselves along the banks and, for several weeks, kept their eyes peeled for the snake in the lake. By August they had logged over twenty sightings and several photographs, a few of which appeared in the *Illustrated London News.* But Mountain's flashiest evidence was a little home movie of something swimming in the loch, although it's impossible to tell just what that something is. When the film was shown to the Linnaean Society of London, there were more shrugs than hugs. "Maybe it is Nessie," they said, "but it could also be an otter, a seal, a whale, or a floating log."

Most photos of Nessie are equally as vague. If you are a believer, the black bumps in the water look like a long, undulating neck; the pear-shaped object looks like a head, reminiscent of the 1950s comic-book character Cecil, the sea serpent. But if you are a skeptic, you see nothing in the photos but blurs—a blurry otter's body, a blurry water-soaked log, blurry floating rubbish.

Now, this would appear to put Nessie into the same category as Bigfoot, but curiously it does not. Nessie is almost respectable; she has the ability to lure such luminaries as the photographic team from *National Geographic*, the staff of the *New York Times*, and researchers from the Academy of Applied Science. They have come with the latest high-tech equipment. Experienced scuba divers have plunged into the murky loch, armed with powerful flashlights and ultrasensitive cameras. The lake has been echo sounded and sonar probed. Everything short of a submarine has been sent to the bottom to search for Nessie. And what does Bigfoot get? Until recently, nothing but amateurs and a little bit of donated money. In the 1980s, a three-day expedition to Loch Ness cost an incredible $1.6 million! Bigfoot hunters practically have to hold bake sales to finance their search parties, and they go armed, not with expensive sonar, but with a few rolls of film and an automatic camera. Clearly, Nessie has more clout. Why?

One reason is Nessie's location. While Bigfoot is believed to range throughout three states and two Canadian provinces, Nessie is held prisoner in a one-mile-by-twenty-two-mile lake. Before the last ice age, Loch Ness was open to the sea, but when the glaciers came down some ten thousand years ago, they forever sealed it off. There are no secret entrances or exits through which Nessie might pass to play hide-and-seek with hunters. So the researchers feel that if she's in there, they'll find her.

Bigfoot, on the other hand, covers a vast territory, which is rugged, remote, and thick with trees. While much of it is government land, much of it is also completely unexplored. To set up even a cursory Bigfoot watch would take a large team and a great deal of money, and because Bigfoot is free to roam wherever he fancies, tracking him is nothing short of a big headache.

Yet another reason why Nessie has the edge on Bigfoot when it comes to credibility is that she often makes an appearance in front of an audience. Bigfoot seems to show himself only to the solitary hiker or camper who then returns to civilization with a wild tale about a hairy ape-man. The eyewitness is excited and babbling, and the listeners—reporters or otherwise—are understandably rolling their eyes in utter disbelief.

But then there's Nessie. She lives in a lake in which scores of people sail every day. There are fishing boats, pleasure craft, and most recently, Nessie charters. On the shores there are picnickers and folks just out for a stroll. The road to Inverness runs smack along the lake, carrying all manner of cars and trucks and bicycles. Peaceful Scottish cottages and inns front the lake, and cozy pubs face the water. When Nessie surfaces, she is seen by four, five, even ten people at a time. Science likes this. There is, one feels, safety in numbers.

Finally, Nessie does not suffer nearly so much from faked photographs and bogus evidence. This is partly because of the sheer numbers of people around Loch Ness. It would be awfully hard to sneak anything large enough to pass for Nessie into the loch without being seen. Furthermore, a mechanical Nessie would have to be watertight, pliant enough to simulate skin, and able to surface and dive at appropriate times. A tall order, to be sure. In 1961, someone built a self-propelled Nessie and floated it in nearby Loch Oich. It looked like a great big bathtub toy and fooled absolutely no one, although it did provide a few laughs.

Not funny at all was a huge bone sent to the *Daily Mail* in 1969. The sender touted it as evidence for Nessie, but science called it an ordinary whalebone. And the police called it robbery. Only a few weeks before it had been on display in a museum in Yorkshire. Certainly, the Nessie hoaxers have something to learn about covering their tracks.

As mentioned, Nessie is occasionally spotted on land where one supposes, she would leave some footprints. Now, footprints are extremely difficult to fake. They are tested and measured and scrutinized because they are considered "hard evidence." So whatever possessed one Nessie hoaxer to send a faked cast to the *Daily Mail* is certainly a mystery. The cast was promptly forwarded to the British Museum, which returned it with a note saying that the print had been made by a stuffed hippo foot.*

Actually, the best chance a Nessie hoaxer has is to fake some photographs. This requires very little preparation, and poor-quality pictures are encouraged. The grainier the film, the blurrier the image, the more open to inter-

---

*This was partly determined by the depth of the print. The shallower the print, the lighter the animal.

pretation and the more successful the photo will be. The pictures that stand the best chance are the ones showing either one or two dark humps in the water with a nice wake behind the humps to simulate movement, or a Brontosaurus-like neck and head, open mouth optional.

Probably the most famous Nessie photograph ever taken was shot by R. K. Wilson in April 1934. This photo stood the test of time for many, many years, partly because it was vague enough to escape close scrutiny and because the photographer was a respected surgeon. Recently, however, sophisticated photographic techniques revealed the photo to be a phony. Ironically, the picture was taken on April 1. . . .

Fakery, flimflam, and doodah, however, are at a minimum in the Nessie camp. Most people who report a sighting really believe they have glimpsed the famed monster. They see a massive shape gliding silently through the tea yellow waters of the loch. They spot one hump, then two, just barely emerging from the murky depths. Their hearts skip beats. They blink their eyes and blink again, and then suddenly the vision is gone. The Scottish lake weaves its legendary magic, and that night the lucky tourist or tenth-generation resident, student or scientist, talks far into the predawn hours. No one exaggerates or embellishes because it is too risky. There are far too many others who have seen the monster, and they know what she looks like. She is some forty-five feet long, although only about half of that is body. Her neck is estimated to be ten feet, her tail fifteen feet. Nessie's shape may be that of a sea serpent or a skinny Brontosaurus with a maximum midsection circumference of just under sixteen feet. Nessie's head is comparatively small and football shaped, and her skin is dark and warty, reminiscent of a reptile. She has prominent flippers set low and well beyond her neck, and she is believed to have very acute hearing.

But does she exist?

There is no question that a good number of eyewitnesses are just plain seeing things. This is not to say that they are hallucinating, only fooled by the tricky physics of the loch. You might think that a glass-smooth sunlit lake would be ideal conditions for viewing monsters, but you would be wrong. The fact is, when sunlight and water get together, they produce mirages. Actually, sunlight can make some very convincing mirages all by itself. Maybe you never have been lost in the desert and seen a bustling metropolis on the sandy horizon, but you almost certainly have been fooled by the old water-on-the-highway trick. During a very warm and glary day, heat from the sun rises off the pavement, creating the illusion that there are puddles of water on the road. On Loch Ness, there is a very interesting phenomenon called the lens effect.

Alex Campbell, whom you met earlier and who has about a dozen genuine sightings under his belt, was tricked one day by the Loch Ness lens effect. At first, Campbell was sure he had spotted Nessie, but later realized that what he actually had seen was a small flock of cormorants. That day, a soft haze hung over the loch. The water droplets in the haze acted like little lenses, magnifying and distorting the image of the cormorants. Sunlight shining through the haze ruined the image even more until a group of long-necked birds turned into a blurry sea serpent. Campbell, a native of Loch Ness, had seen the phenomenon many times before, and he wasn't fooled for long. But what about the people who know absolutely nothing about physics and lens effects? What about the average tourist who comes to Loch Ness hoping to catch that precious glimpse of Nessie?

Millicent Throbheart scans the loch with her $29.95 binoculars on sale for $17.88. Suddenly, she spots movement in the water, and her heart begins to beat wildly.

"Oh my, oh my, oh my!" she exclaims, and twiddles the focus.

Her gentlemen friend, Ernest Chowder, strains his bespectacled eyes. "Do you see something?" he cries. His heart begins to beat, too.

"Oh my," says Millicent again for emphasis. "I see a shape. A dark shape." She jumps just the tiniest bit off the ground and thrusts the binoculars at Ernest. "Is it she?" she asks.

Ernest removes his glasses and squints into the eyepieces.

"Hurry, Ernest, hurry!"

"Well, now, you're making me nervous. . . ."

And then, "Oh, my goodness, Millicent!"

Millicent's pulse is 125. She is beside herself with excitement. She is framing her tale right now for all her friends back in Hunkee Doree, Nebraska.

Ernest is breathing faster. "Yes, yes, yes!" he gasps. "It's the monster! Oh, Millicent, it's the monster!"

Together they stare at the rippling vision on the lake. They look for the three humps, just as the guidebook says to. They search for the long, undulating neck and the small head, and of course, they see it all. When the monster vanishes into the waves from a passing boat, they run like lightning to report their wondrous sighting. And when they are gone, the rotted log bobs to the surface once again.

Certainly a large number of sightings are in reality blurry mirages made even worse, ironically, by perfect weather conditions. They are flotsam and jetsam that are so far away from the viewer that they cannot be identified clearly. They are rising air currents exaggerated by wishful thinking. And they are photographs taken, perhaps, in not such good faith, of the intersecting wakes of two motorboats. It has been suggested that a full 80 to 90 percent of all Nessie sightings are bogus.

But there must be something going on at Loch Ness because the Scottish monster has captured the attention of some pretty respectable parties.

In 1970, Robert H. Rines of the Academy of Applied Science in Boston decided to go on a Nessie hunt. The creature had caught both his imagination and interest, and despite the insistent voices of the skeptics, Rines felt an aquatic creature like Nessie could conceivably exist. Nessie's characteristics were not outside the laws of biology the way, say, those of a mermaid would be. So Rines visited Loch Ness that summer and invited sonar expert Martin Klein to join him.

Rines used a 16mm camera and a strobe-light apparatus that he dropped into the loch from a small boat. At preset intervals, the camera shutter would trip and cause the strobe to flash. Rines hoped his strobe would be powerful enough to light up the sediment-filled waters of the loch. He knew the picture quality would probably be poor; the loch is simply too dark, and the visibility is worse than terrible. But Rines felt that if a large animal were down there, he stood a good chance of capturing at least some part of it on film.

Klein's equipment was a sonar machine, which operates by bouncing sound waves off objects. Usually Klein would trail his sonar machine in the water from the stern of a boat, but to track Nessie, he decided to keep the machine stationary. That way, fixed objects on the bottom—logs, rocks, and debris—constantly would be recorded by the sonar, giving Klein a picture of the loch floor. But when a moving object passed through the sonar trap, it would show up as something new, something that had not been there before.

During that first summer, Rines struck out with his camera, but Klein hit the jackpot. His sonar recorded a massive solid object that was unquestionably in motion. Based on its "echo," Klein estimated the object's size as "somewhere in the neighborhood of ten to fifty times as big as the other fish we had seen."

Excited by the find, Klein continued to monitor the water and, thirty minutes later, recorded the object again. Its signature on the printout was unmistakable. After a third pass within fifteen minutes of the second one, Klein was certain he had something that would make headlines.

Rines now was convinced. He returned to the loch the following summer with high hopes but came up empty. Undaunted, however, he was back again in 1972, and that's when he got his money's worth for all the film he had used. The pictures were black-and-white and very grainy, but there was no mistaking the object. It was an enormous fin, and it was moving.

But it was Rines's 1975 expedition that really made waves—all the way up to Britain's House of Commons.

As usual, Rines had dropped his camera and strobe into the loch. As he waited, perhaps not so patiently, the shutter clicked again and again and in all produced two thousand photos that summer. Some time later, Rines unwound the film spool in front of a light source for a quick look. He saw virtually nothing. The frames showed gray, gray, and more gray. Occasionally there seemed to be changes in the lighting, but certainly no water monster reared its ugly head and made scary faces at the camera.

Rines felt, however, that he needed expert eyes to carefully scrutinize the photos, so he called on his friend Charlie Wyckoff who warmed to the task almost immediately. Like Rines, Wyckoff was underwhelmed the first time he looked at the pictures, but by the third and fourth run-throughs, his eyebrows began to rise. He was seeing a funny kind of mottling in some of the pictures. This could not be sand and pebbles from the bottom of the loch because the camera had been dropped only forty feet. It had hung suspended, like a fishing line.

Wyckoff instinctively pulled his chair closer to the mysterious pictures. He squinted in intense concentration. And gradually, Wyckoff began to see. Unbelievably, Rines's camera had photographed an enormous head.

The head seemed to be glaring into the lens. Its huge mouth gaped wide; its nostrils—mistakenly thought to be eyes by Rines—flared menacingly. Two protuberances, like stubby horns or undeveloped antler buds, sat atop the head, giving the creature the classic look of a sea serpent. Other frames showed part of the animal's body and a section of a thick neck that Wyckoff later estimated to be nearly five feet around. The body was well in excess of twenty feet long, a number Wyckoff calculated based on how far the animal was from the camera and the lighting angle. This astonishing evidence seemed to prove almost beyond a shadow of a doubt that there was, indeed, a large, aquatic animal living in Loch Ness.

It did not take long before the press got wind of all of this and Rines was hounded. He kept silent, however (no easy task), until his formal presentation to the House of Commons on the evening of December 10, 1975. Along with British naturalist Sir Peter Scott, Rines declared Nessie official by bestowing upon her a scientific name—*Nessiteras rhombopteryx*. This translates as "Ness wonder with the diamond-shaped fin"—a little unwieldy but certainly descriptive. Nessie's name was not fluff. Once she had been classified in the correct scientific manner, she earned the right to be protected under the law. This, few would doubt, was essential, especially if Nessie were the only one of her kind.

Never before had so many esteemed people fought for Nessie. Never before had the evidence been so strong. But the scientific community refused to bless the proceedings. Not enough clear and unmistakable evidence, they said. They did concede that there was something in the loch, something that could not be explained, but no one would say that it was *Nessiteras rhombopteryx*. In the zoology books and the halls of marine biology, the Loch Ness monster still did not exist.

May 30, 1976, and Rines was back at the loch. This time, he and his colleagues, who included Charlie and Helen Wyckoff, Martin Klein, and *New York Times* science editor John Noble Wilford, were armed to the teeth. It took them an entire day to set up all their equipment, and it was not until late at night that Rines was finally able to send his camera deep into the loch. The camera had been set to take a picture every fifteen seconds, producing some two thousand photographs every eight hours. All through the dark night, the strobe flashed a muted yellow in the dingy, tea-colored waters. In the background, Urquhart Castle rose up like something straight out of a Scottish epic, its stone battlements and great turrets harboring the ghosts of long ago. It was, indeed, a fitting place for a monster hunt.

In addition to Rines's trusty 16mm camera, there were a Polaroid instant camera, two 35mm stereo cameras, and a TV camera. There were three separate strobes and a sonar hookup. Rines was determined that the beast would not escape. But throughout that summer of 1976, the beast did escape. There were plenty of sightings, of course. With the media on hand nearly every step of the way, there was bound to be a frenzy of Nessie-mania. Some claimed they saw the animal making her way across the road. Others insisted she had burst from the lake, nearly overturning their boat. Even a couple of the expedition team members thought they had had a brush with Nessie. But as for pictures—good close-up shots of an unidentified animal in the loch . . . nothing.

There were, however, some very intriguing finds. First, Klein's sonar picked up an extraordinary configuration of stone circles on the floor of the loch. Nicknamed "Kleinhenge I" after the famous stone monoliths of Stonehenge in England, the circles look remarkably nestlike. We are all familiar with the twig-and-leaf nests of birds, but a number of animals build stone nests. Patiently, they roll rocks and large pebbles along the ground to the chosen nest site, fashioning a circle big enough to accommodate the forthcoming eggs. This is not to say that the Loch Ness stones are nesting sites for a population of Nessies—surely they aren't—but they do raise a lot of questions about both the geology of the loch and the history of the area.

The British Isles are home to over nine hundred stone sites. The stones vary in their sizes and shapes (some are monstrous stone slabs weighing several tones), but nearly all have been arranged to form huge circles. Historians and archaeologists believe that the sites were used as astronomical observatories or, at the very least, calendars. If the stone circles under Loch Ness are similar, then one of two things must have occurred: Either the early Scots were terrific skin divers or at some point in time Loch Ness was dry.

Klein hopes that his discovery will lure other scientists to the loch and that their explorations will add more pieces to the Nessie puzzle. If a large prehistoric beast is swimming around in a sealed-off lake, one of the biggest questions that needs to be addressed is, How in blazes did the thing get in there in the first place? Geological investigations may uncover the answer.

Klein's sonar also caught the dramatic echo of a large, unknown object resting three hundred feet down on the floor of the loch. Dubbed "the average plesiosaur,"* it measures about thirty feet long, but just exactly what this plesiosaur-thing might be, Klein cannot say. A more recent three-day expedition to the loch yielded three V-shaped sonar blips at a depth of six hundred twenty feet. Another picture of Klein's plesiosaur? Or three more?

The shadows are long at Loch Ness. Deep within the cold and forbidding waters something hides from the light of the powerful strobes. Silently it moves its great bulk into the yawning mouth of one of the many submarine caves. And there the thing waits for the little submersible that will surely come one day. It will be lowered into the loch as it was lowered into the seven-mile depth of the Mariana Trench in the Pacific. Then the explorers inside will guide the minisubmarine through the silt-studded waters on what surely would be the definitive quest for Nessie. But maybe they will not find her even then. Maybe she will remain one of nature's most engaging mysteries.

Maybe the search will never really end. . . .

---

*Plesiosaurs were large marine reptiles that lived during the Mesozoic era. They had great flippers and long, sleek bodies, which measured up to forty-six feet long.

Selected Bibliography

Books

Bakker, Robert T. *The Dinosaur Heresies.* New York: William Morrow, 1986.

Bauer, Henry. *The Enigma of Loch Ness.* Champaign, Ill.: University of Illinois Press, 1986.

Breland, Osmond. *Animal Life and Lore.* New York: Harper and Row, 1972.

Corliss, William R. *A Handbook of Biological Mysteries.* Glen Arm, Md.: The Sourcebook Project, 1981.

Erlich, Paul, and Anne Erlich. *Extinction.* New York: Random House, 1981.

Napier, John. *Bigfoot.* New York: E. P. Dutton, 1973.

Orr, Robert. *Animals in Migration.* New York: Macmillan, 1970.

Raup, David M. *The Mystery of Animal Migration.* New York: Hill & Wang, 1968.

Shockley, Myra. *Still Living?* New York: Thames and Hudson, 1983.

Stout, William. *The Dinosaur.* New York: Bantam Books, 1981.

――――. *Mysteries of the Unexplained.* Pleasantville, N.Y.: Reader's Digest, 1981.

Periodicals

Anderson, D. "New Arms, New Bodies." *Science Digest* 89 (1981): 51.

Angler, N. "Did Comets Kill the Dinosaurs?" *Time* 125 (1985): 72–74+.

"Animals as Earthquake Predictors." U.S. Geological Survey, Books and Open File Reports, Denver, Colo.

Begley, S. "How Animals Winter Weather." *Newsweek* 101 (1983): 43.

Borgens, R. B. "Mice Regrow the Tip of Their Foretoes." *Science* 217 (1982): 747–50.

Bowser, H. "Indestructible!" *Science Digest,* May 1981, 49–51.

Davidson, M. and N. Ponnamperum. "Benefits of the Big Sleep," *Science Digest* 90 (1982): 103

"The Great Extinction: What Happened and Why?" *Science Digest,* March 1978, 25–27.

Fleming, C. B. "How Do Animals Hibernate?" *Science '84* 5 (1984): 28+.

Heller, C. and R. Berger. "Origin of Winter Sleep." *Natural History* 89 (1980): 6+.

"Hibernation." *Science Digest* 84 (1978): 96–97.

Huyghe, P. "The Search for Bigfoot." *Science Digest* 92 (1984): 56–59+.

Kelsey, P. "Hibernation and Winter Withdrawal." *Conservationist* 23 (1968): 20–27.

———. "Seven Sleeperz-z-z." *Conservationist* 32 (1978): 28–32.

Kerr, R. A., "Quake Prediction Under Way in Earnest." *Science* 233 (1986): 520.

Meredith, D. "Healing with Electricity." *Science Digest* 89 (1981): 52–57.

Morgan, D. "How Animals Predict Earthquakes." *Science Digest* 89 (1981): 92–95+.

Singer, W. H. "From the Body Shop: Giving the Mechanics Their 'Pink Slips.'" *Sciquest* 53 (1980): 5–9.

Sloan, R. E., et al. "Cretaceous-Tertiary Dinosaur Extinction." *Science* 234 (1986): 1170–75.

Index